THE BOOK OF
Useless
Information

THE BOOK OF
USELESS
INFORMATION

**NOEL BOTHAM AND THE
USELESS INFORMATION SOCIETY**

A PERIGEE BOOK

A PERIGEE BOOK
Published by the Penguin Group
Penguin Group (USA) Inc.

While the author has made every effort to provide accurate telephone numbers and Internet addresses at the time of publication, neither the publisher nor the author assumes any responsibility for errors, or for changes that occur after publication. Further, publisher does not have any control over and does not assume any responsibility for author or third-party websites or their content.

THE BOOK OF USELESS INFORMATION

This special edition has been adapted for all ages.

Proprietary ISBN: 978-1-101-94946-7

An application to register this book for cataloging has been submitted to the Library of Congress.

PRINTED IN THE UNITED STATES OF AMERICA

4   6   8   9   7   5   3

Members of The Useless Information Society

CONTENTS

INTRODUCTION

OH, but just how useless is useless? There, as Shakespeare observes in Act III, Scene I, of *The Oxford Dictionary of Quotations*, is the rub.

For instance, the news that flamingos can only eat with their heads upside down, while of more than passing interest to a female flamingo teaching her fledglings to eat up their shrimp, is of little use to a human being trained to sit up at a table and employ a knife and fork. Yet suppose someone made one a present of a flamingo, and it persisted in eating with its head upside down. You could spend a fortune on vet bills before learning that, in flamingo circles, that is the way it is done.

So we have to tread carefully. There have to be checks and balances. At our Useless Information Society summit meetings, we have these in the form of our formidable resident beadle, the distinguished jazz musician Kennie Clayton. If Mr. Beadle Clayton judges that an item may be

put to use in the community, he solemnly bangs his cere-
monial staff and it is ruled out of order. There is no appeal,
although barracking and cries of "Rubbish!" are permitted.

An exception is sometimes made of material that may
be of use to a biographer. Thus, when I learned from a
newspaper cutting that Marilyn Monroe had six toes, I ea-
gerly produced this nugget at the next Useless Information soirée in the confident belief that, with so many
Marilyn biographers still trawling, it would get under the
net. So it proved. What I hadn't bargained for was that one
of our more pedantic members—and we have a few—
would seek to have the item barred on purely arithmetical
grounds, on the basis that in total she must have had
eleven toes at least.

The only other transgression is that of being boring. At
the society's earliest meetings, a few members misunder-
stood the nature of uselessness and came up with such
conversation-stoppers as that the Mississippi is 1,171 miles
long or, for those who prefer it, 1,884 kilometers. We
useless information aficionados are not interested in the
length of rivers, a fact that is traditionally conveyed to the
offender with elaborate yawns and shouts of "Boring!"
Tell us, however, that in the Nuuanu Valley of Honolulu
there is a river that flows upward, and our eyes light up.

Mr. Gradgrind, in the same volume as the Bard's
"There's the rub" gag, observes, "Facts alone are wanted
in life." That is the policy of The Useless Information Society. It could be our motto.

But there are facts and *facts*. Useless information, as may be judged from this modest volume, is not in the same category as trivia, as in Trivial Pursuit. We do not care about any of that *Guinness World Records* kind of stuff. All our information has to pass the "Not a Lot of People Know That" test, preceded by gasps of surprise and, in extreme cases, followed by wild applause.

If we can send our fellow members home with their heads reeling under the weight of a cornucopia of entirely useless and out-of-the-way facts, then our deliberations will not have been in vain.

Keith Waterhouse

THE USELESS INFORMATION MASCOT

It is estimated that millions of trees are planted by forgetful squirrels.

Squirrels can climb trees faster than they can run on the ground.

Squirrels may live fifteen or twenty years in captivity, but their life span in the wild is often only about one year. They fall prey to disease, malnutrition, predators, cars, and humans.

A squirrel cannot contract or carry the rabies virus.

THE BOOK OF
USELESS
INFORMATION

HALL OF FAME

HAIL TO THE CHIEFS

All U.S. presidents have worn glasses; some of them just didn't like to be seen wearing them in public.

There has never been a president from the Air Force or Marine Corps, although Ronald Reagan was in the Army Air Corps.

More presidents have been born in the state of Virginia than in any other state.

No president has been an only child.

David Rice Atchinson was president of the United States for exactly one day.

🌰 CURIOUS GEORGE

George Washington is the only man whose birthday is a legal holiday in every state as of a few years ago.

George Washington was deathly afraid of being buried alive. After he died, he wanted to be laid out for three days just to be sure he was dead.

George Washington's false teeth were made of whale bone.

George Washington had to borrow money to go to his own inauguration.

Thomas Jefferson anonymously submitted design plans for the White House. They were rejected. He was the first president to be inaugurated in Washington, D.C.

Thomas Jefferson, John Adams, and James Monroe all died on July 4. Jefferson and Adams died at practically the same minute of the same day.

John Quincy Adams owned a pet alligator, which he kept in the East Room of the White House.

John Quincy Adams took his last skinny dip in the Potomac on his seventy-ninth birthday.

Andrew Jackson was the only president to believe that the world is flat.

The longest inaugural address by a U.S. president was given by William Henry Harrison. It was one hour, forty-five minutes long during an intense snowstorm. One month later, he died of pneumonia.

John Tyler had fifteen children.

Millard Fillmore's mother feared he may have been mentally retarded.

James Buchanan is said to have had the neatest handwriting of all the presidents. He was the only unmarried president.

Andrew Johnson was the only self-educated tailor. He is the only president to make his own clothes and those of his cabinet.

Ulysses S. Grant had the boyhood nickname "Useless."

🐿 HONEST ABE

Abraham Lincoln had a wart on his face.

Abraham Lincoln's mother died when the family dairy cow ate poisonous mushrooms and Mrs. Lincoln drank the milk.

Abraham Lincoln had a nervous breakdown in 1836.

Abraham Lincoln's famous Gettysburg Address consisted of just 272 words.

Before winning the presidential election in 1860, Abraham Lincoln lost eight elections for various offices.

A short time before Abraham Lincoln's assassination, he dreamed he was going to die, and he related his dream to the Senate. He died in the same bed that had been occupied by his assassin, John Wilkes Booth. His ghost is said to haunt the White House.

The annual White House Easter egg roll was started by Rutherford B. Hayes in 1878.

James Garfield could write Latin with one hand and Greek with the other—simultaneously!

Grover Cleveland was a draft dodger. He hired someone to enter the service in his place, for which he was ridiculed by his political opponent, James G. Blaine. It was soon discovered, however, that Blaine had done the same thing himself.

TEDDY TIDBITS

In 1912, after being shot in the chest, Theodore Roosevelt finished a speech he was delivering before he accepted any medical help.

Theodore Roosevelt was the first to announce to the world that Maxwell House coffee is "Good to the last drop."

Theodore Roosevelt wrote thirty-seven books.

Theodore Roosevelt's mother and first wife died on the same day in 1884. He himself died from an infected tooth.

William Taft got stuck in his bathtub on his Inauguration Day and had to be pried out by his attendants. He had a special, reinforced steel dining chair.

Woodrow Wilson wrote all of his speeches in longhand. He is the only president who has held a Ph.D. degree.

Herbert Hoover was the first U.S. president to have a telephone in his office.

When First Lady Eleanor Roosevelt received an alarming number of threatening letters soon after her husband became president at the height of the Depression, the Secret Service insisted that she carry a pistol in her purse.

Harry Truman's middle name was just S and was not short for anything. His parents could not decide between two different names beginning with S.

John F. Kennedy could read four newspapers in twenty minutes.

John F. Kennedy's rocking chair was auctioned off for $442,000.

Pluto, the astrological symbol for death, was directly above Dallas when JFK was born.

Lyndon B. Johnson was the first president of the United States to wear contact lenses.

Richard Nixon left instructions for "California, Here I Come" to be the last piece of music played (slowly and softly) were he to die in office.

Richard Nixon's favorite drink was a dry martini.

Richard Nixon was the first U.S. president to visit Moscow.

Gerald Ford was once a male model.

Jimmy Carter is a speed reader (two thousand words per minute).

Jimmy Carter was the first U.S. president born in a hospital. He had an operation for hemorrhoids while he was in office.

REAGANISMS

Ronald Reagan once wore a Nazi uniform while acting in a film during his Hollywood days.

Ronald Reagan married his first wife, Jane Wyman, at Forest Lawn Cemetery in Glendale, California.

Ronald Reagan sent out the Army photographer who first discovered Marilyn Monroe.

Ronald Reagan was the only divorced president, and he was the only president to be head of a labor union.

Bill Clinton was the first left-handed U.S. president to serve two terms.

CRIMINAL MINDS

Al Capone's famous scars (which earned him the nickname "Scarface") were from an attack. The brother of a girl he had insulted attacked him with a knife, leaving him with three distinctive scars.

Al Capone's business card said he was a used furniture dealer. His brother was a town sheriff.

While in Alcatraz, Al Capone was inmate 85.

> Behram, an Indian thug, holds the record for most mur-
> ders by a single individual. He strangled 931 people be-
> tween 1790 and 1840 with a piece of yellow and white
> cloth called a ruhmal. The most by a woman is 610, by
> Countess Erzsebet Bathory of Hungary.

Fidel Castro was once a star baseball player for the University of Havana in the 1940s.

> Leon Trotsky, the seminal Russian Communist, was
> assassinated in Mexico with an ice pick.

Josef Stalin's left foot had webbed toes, and his left arm
was noticeably shorter than his right arm.

THE OTHER KENNEDYS

Robert Kennedy was killed in the Ambassador Hotel, the
same hotel that housed Marilyn Monroe's first modeling
agency.

> While at Harvard University, Edward Kennedy was
> suspended for cheating on a Spanish exam.

LOUIS, LOUIS

Louis IV of France had a stomach the size of two regular stomachs.

Louis XIV bathed once a year. He had forty personal wigmakers and almost one thousand wigs.

THE ROYAL WE

The Queen of England has two birthdays—one real and one official.

The shortest British monarch was Charles I, who was four foot, nine inches.

Catherine the Great relaxed by being tickled.

Princess Grace of Monaco was once on the board of 20th Century Fox.

The royal house of Saudi Arabia has close to ten thousand princes and princesses.

While performing her duties as queen, Cleopatra sometimes wore a fake beard.

King Tut's tomb contained four coffins. The third coffin was made from twenty-five hundred pounds of gold, and in today's market is worth approximately $13 million.

Peter the Great executed his wife's lover and forced her to keep her lover's head in a jar of alcohol in her bedroom.

The German kaiser Wilhelm II had a withered arm and often hid the fact by posing with his hand resting on a sword or by holding a glove.

The Mongol emperor Genghis Khan's original name was Temuji. He started out as a goatherder.

Alexander the Great was an epileptic. He was tutored by Aristotle.

Augustus Caesar had achluophobia—the fear of sitting in the dark.

Catherine de Medici was the first woman in Europe to use tobacco. She took it in a mixture of snuff.

GOD SAVE THE QUEEN

Six of Queen Victoria's grandchildren were married to rulers of countries—England, Russia, Germany, Sweden, Norway, and Romania. Queen Victoria's native language was German.

The first thing Queen Victoria did after her coronation was to remove her bed from her mother's room.

One of Queen Victoria's children gave her a bustle for Christmas that played "God Save the Queen" when she sat down.

All of Queen Anne's seventeen children died before she did.

Anne Boleyn, Queen Elizabeth I's mother, had six fingers on one hand.

Elizabeth I suffered from anthophobia—a fear of roses.

Princess Anne competed in the 1976 Summer Olympics.

Queen Berengaria (1191 c.e.) of England never lived in nor visited England.

ARTISTIC ENDEAVORS

The famous painting *Whistler's Mother* was once bought from a pawn shop.

The *Mona Lisa* was completed in 1503. It was stolen from the Louvre on August 21, 1911.

A Flemish artist is responsible for the world's smallest painting in history. It is a picture of a miller and his mill, and it was painted onto a grain of corn.

Artist Constantino Brumidi fell from the dome of the U.S. Capitol while painting a mural around the rim. He died four months later.

Leonardo da Vinci spent twelve years painting the *Mona Lisa's* lips. He could also write with one hand and draw with the other at the same time.

On a trip to the South Sea Islands, French painter Paul Gauguin stopped off briefly in Central America, where he worked as a laborer on the Panama Canal.

Salvador Dalí once arrived at an art exhibition in a limousine filled with turnips.

When young and impoverished, Pablo Picasso kept warm by burning his own paintings.

Michelangelo carved the famed Medici tombs in Florence.

🌰 GOGH CRAZY

Vincent van Gogh decided to become an artist when he was twenty-seven years old.

Van Gogh cut off his left ear. His *Self-Portrait with Bandaged Ear* shows the right one bandaged because he painted his mirror image.

During his entire life, van Gogh sold only one painting, *Red Vineyard at Arles*.

Van Gogh committed suicide while painting *Wheat Field with Crows*.

BRAINIACS

Alexander Graham Bell made a talking doll that said "Mama" when he was a young boy in Scotland. He never telephoned his wife or mother. They were both deaf.

Aristotle thought blood cooled the brain.

Despite his great scientific and artistic achievement, Leonardo da Vinci was most proud of his ability to bend iron with his bare hands.

Jeremy Bentham, a British philosopher who died in 1832, left his entire estate to the London Hospital, provided that his body was allowed to preside over its board meetings. His skeleton was clothed and fitted with a wax mask of his face. It was present at the meeting for ninety-two years and can still be viewed there.

Thomas Edison had a collection of more than five thousand birds. He once saved a boy from the path of an oncoming locomotive.

NEWTONIAN PRINCIPLES

Isaac Newton was an ordained priest in the Church of England.

Isaac Newton was only twenty-three years old when he discovered the law of universal gravitation.

Isaac Newton dropped out of school when he was a teenager.

Isaac Newton was a Member of Parliament.

Nobody knows where Voltaire's body is. It was stolen in the nineteenth century and has never been recovered. The theft was discovered in 1864, when the tomb was opened and found empty.

Sigmund Freud had a morbid fear of ferns.

At age sixteen, Confucius was a corn inspector.

🎵 RELATIVITY SPEAKING

Albert Einstein couldn't speak fluently when he was nine. His parents thought he might be mentally retarded.

In 1921, Einstein was awarded the Nobel Prize in Physics for his work with the photoelectric effect.

Einstein was offered the presidency of Israel in 1952.

When Einstein was inducted as an American, he attended the ceremony without socks.

Einstein's last words were in German. Because the attending nurse did not understand German, his last words will never be known.

THAT EXPLAINS IT

Hitler and Napoleon both had only one testicle.

A LITTLE EGO

Napoleon Bonaparte was afraid of cats.

Napoleon conducted his battle plans in a sandbox.

Napoleon favored mathematicians and physical scientists but excluded humanists from his circle, believing them to be troublemakers.

Napoleon had his servants wear his boots to break them in before he wore them.

LARGER THAN LIFE

Attila the Hun was a dwarf. Pepin the Short, Aesop, Gregory the Tours, Charles III of Naples, and the Pasha Hussain were all shorter than three and a half feet tall.

BIG BEN

Benjamin Franklin wanted the turkey, not the eagle, to be the U.S. national bird.

Benjamin Franklin was the first head of the United States Post Office.

Benjamin Franklin's peers did not give him the assignment of writing the Declaration of Independence because they feared he would conceal a joke in it.

DID IT RUN WINDOWS?

Bill Gates's first business was Traff-O-Data, a company that created machines that recorded the number of cars passing a given point on a road.

WE LIKE TO CALL HIM "ECCENTRIC"

Henry Ford believed in reincarnation and flatly stated that history is bunk.

GLOBETROTTERS

Marco Polo was born on the Croatian island of Korcula (pronounced *Kor-chu-la*).

Christopher Columbus had blond hair.

American explorer Richard Byrd once spent five months alone in Antarctica.

Harry Houdini was the first person to fly an airplane on the continent of Australia.

THAT'S ENTERTAINMENT

A ROSE BY ANY OTHER NAME

Bruce Willis's real name is Walter.

Cher's real name is Cherilyn La Pierre.

Hulk Hogan's real name is Terry Bollea.

Ice Cube's real name is O'Shea Jackson.

John Wayne's real name was Marion Morrison.

Judy Garland's real name was Frances Gumm.

Tom Cruise's real name is Thomas Mapother.

Tina Turner's real name is Annie Mae Bullock.

Vanilla Ice's real name is Robert Van Winkle.

Albert Brooks's real name is Albert Einstein.

Ralph Lauren's real name is Ralph Lifshitz.

Jim Carrey's middle name is Eugene.

Keanu Reeves's first name means "cool breeze over the mountains" in Hawaiian.

FAMILY TIES

Warren Beatty and Shirley MacLaine are brother and sister.

Sophia Loren's sister was once married to the son of the Italian dictator Benito Mussolini.

Julie Nixon, daughter of Richard Nixon, married David Eisenhower, grandson of Dwight Eisenhower.

Humphrey Bogart was related to Princess Diana, according to U.S. genealogists.

Tom Hanks is related to Abraham Lincoln.

I'M READY FOR MY CLOSE-UP

Andy Garcia was a conjoined twin.

Arnold Schwarzenegger bought the first Hummer manufactured for civilian use, in 1992. The vehicle weighed in at 6,300 pounds and was seven feet wide. He also paid $772,500 for President John F. Kennedy's golf clubs at a 1996 auction.

Tommy Lee Jones and Vice President Al Gore were freshmen roommates at Harvard.

Sarah Bernhardt played a thirteen-year-old Juliet when she was seventy years old.

Although he starred in many gangster films, James Cagney started his career as a chorus boy.

As a child, Jodie Foster appeared in Coppertone commercials.

Bruce Lee was so fast that his films actually had to be slowed down so audiences could see his moves.

The first actress to appear on a postage stamp was Grace Kelly.

Tom Cruise at one time wanted to be a priest.

Peter Falk, who played Columbo, has a glass eye.

Peter Mayhew, who played Chewbacca in the first three *Star Wars* movies, was a hospital porter in London before starring as the Wookie.

Shirley Temple made $1 million by age ten.

Keanu Reeves once managed a pasta shop in Toronto.

Melanie Griffith's mother is actress Tippi Hedren, best known for her lead role in Alfred Hitchcock's *The Birds*.

Alfred Hitchcock did not have a belly button.

Rita Moreno was the first and only entertainer to have received all four of America's top entertainment industry awards: the Oscar, the Emmy, the Tony, and the Grammy.

James Doohan, who played Lt. Commander Montgomery Scott on *Star Trek*, was missing his entire middle finger on his right hand.

Jack Nicholson appeared on *The Andy Griffith Show* twice.

Telly Savalas and Louis Armstrong died on their birthdays.

Orson Welles is buried in an olive orchard on a ranch owned by his friend, matador Antonio Ordonez, in Seville, Spain.

Kathleen Turner was the voice of Jessica Rabbit in the movie *Who Framed Roger Rabbit?* Amy Irving was her singing voice.

James Dean died in a Porsche Spyder.

Sylvia Miles had the shortest performance ever nominated for an Oscar with her role in *Midnight Cowboy.* Her entire role lasted only six minutes.

Katharine Hepburn is the only person to win four Oscars for Best Actress.

Clark Gable used to shower more than four times a day.

Elizabeth Taylor appeared on the cover of *Life* magazine more than anyone else.

MAKE 'EM LAUGH

Charlie Chaplin started in show business at age five. He was so popular during the 1920s and 1930s he received more than 73,000 letters in just two days during a visit to London.

Charlie Chaplin once won third prize in a Charlie Chaplin look-alike contest.

Howdy Doody had forty-eight freckles. His twin brother was named Double Doody.

Dan Aykroyd's cone head from *Saturday Night Live* was auctioned off for $2,200.

Roseanne Barr used to be an opening act for Julio Iglesias.

I WANNA HOLD YOUR HAND

The Beatles featured two left-handed members: Paul, whom everyone saw holding his Hoffner bass left-handed, and Ringo, whose left-handedness is at least partially to blame for his "original" drumming style.

The Beatles performed their first U.S. concert in Carnegie Hall.

The Beatles song "A Day in the Life" ends with a note sustained for forty seconds.

The Beatles song "Dear Prudence" was written about Mia Farrow's sister, Prudence, when she wouldn't come out and play with Mia and The Beatles at a religious retreat in India.

The license plate number on the Volkswagen that appeared on the cover of The Beatles' album *Abbey Road* is 281F.

"When I'm Sixty-Four" was the first song to be recorded for the *Sgt. Pepper* album. "Within You Without You" was the last.

When John Lennon divorced Julian Lennon's mother, Paul McCartney composed "Hey Jude" to cheer up Julian.

John Lennon's first girlfriend was named Thelma Pickles.

John Lennon's middle name was Winston.

Ringo Starr was born during a World War II air raid.

ONE-MAN SHOW

An eighteenth-century German named Matthew Birchinger, known as The Little Man of Nuremberg, played four musical instruments, including the bagpipes; was an expert calligrapher; and was the most famous stage magician of his day. He performed tricks with the cup and balls that have never been explained. Yet Birchinger had no hands, legs, or thighs, and he was shorter than twenty-nine inches tall.

INSTRUMENTAL VERSION

The bagpipe was originally made from the whole skin of a dead sheep. Carnegie Mellon University offers bagpiping as a major.

A penny whistle has six finger holes.

The tango originated as a dance between two men for partnering practice.

The harmonica is the world's most popular instrument.

There are more than thirty-three thousand radio stations around the world.

A single violin is made of seventy separate pieces of wood.

Glass flutes do not expand with humidity, so their owners are spared the nuisance of tuning them.

The first U.S. disco was the Whisky A Go-Go in Los Angeles.

Gandhi took dance and music lessons in his late teens.

CLASSICALLY SPEAKING

More than one hundred descendants of Johann Sebastian Bach have been cathedral organists.

When Beethoven was a child, he made such a poor impression on his music teachers that he was pronounced hopeless as a composer.

Beethoven's *Fifth* was the first symphony to include trombones.

Every time Beethoven sat down to write music, he poured ice water over his head.

Mozart's real name was Johannes Chrysostomus Wolfgangus Theophilus Mozart.

Mozart wrote the nursery rhyme "Twinkle Twinkle, Little Star" at the age of five.

Mozart is buried in an unmarked pauper's grave.

PLAY THAT FUNKY MUSIC

At age forty-seven, The Rolling Stones' bassist, Bill Wyman, began a relationship with thirteen-year-old Mandy Smith, with her mother's blessing. Six years later, they were married, but the marriage only lasted a year. Not long after, Bill's thirty-year-old son, Stephen, married Mandy's mother, age forty-six. That made Stephen a stepfather to his former stepmother. If Bill and Mandy had remained married, Stephen would have been his father's father-in-law and his own grandfather.

The music hall entertainer Nosmo King derived his stage name from a NO SMOKING sign.

Nick Mason is the only member of Pink Floyd to appear on all the band's albums.

The naked baby on the cover of Nirvana's album *Nevermind* is named Spencer Eldon.

The 1980s song "Rosanna" was written about actress Rosanna Arquette.

The B-52s were named after a 1950s hairdo.

The band Duran Duran got their name from a character in the 1968 Jane Fonda movie *Barbarella*.

The bestselling Christmas single of all time is Bing Crosby's "White Christmas."

The first CD pressed in the United States was Bruce Springsteen's *Born in the USA*.

The Grateful Dead were once called The Warlocks.

The only member of the band ZZ Top to not have a beard has the last name Beard.

There is a band named A Life-Threatening Buttocks Condition.

The song with the longest title is "I'm a Cranky Old Yank in a Clanky Old Tank on the Streets of Yokohama with My Honolulu Mama Doin' Those Beat-O, Beat-O Flat-On-My-Seat-O, Hirohito Blues," written by Hoagy Carmichael. He later claimed the song title ended with "Yank" and the rest was a joke.

Tommy James got the inspiration to write his number-one hit "Mony Mony" while he was in a New York hotel looking at the Mutual of New York building's neon sign flashing repeatedly: M-O-N-Y.

ABBA got its name by taking the first letter from each of the band members' names (Agnetha, Bjorn, Benny, and Anni-frid).

> The opera singer Enrico Caruso practiced in the bath, while accompanied by a pianist in a nearby room.

Enrico Caruso and Roy Orbison were the only tenors in the twentieth century capable of hitting the note E over high C.

> The song "I Am the Walrus" by John Lennon was inspired by a two-tone police siren.

Aerosmith's "Dude Looks Like a Lady" was written about Vince Neil of Mötley Crüe.

> Andy Warhol created The Rolling Stones' emblem depicting the big tongue. It first appeared on the cover of the *Sticky Fingers* album.

"Happy Birthday to You" is the most often sung song in America.

LONG LIVE THE KING

Elvis Presley had a twin brother named Garon, who died at birth. Elvis's middle name was spelled Aron in honor of his brother.

Elvis loved to eat meatloaf. He weighed 230 pounds at the time of his death.

Elvis failed his music class in school.

Elvis never gave an encore.

Elvis was once appointed Special Agent of the Bureau of Narcotics and Dangerous Drugs. According to Elvis's autopsy, he had ten different drugs in his body at the time of his death.

Frank Sinatra was once quoted as saying that rock 'n' roll was only played by "cretinous goons."

Jim Morrison of The Doors was the first rock star to be arrested onstage.

Mr. Mojo Risin is an anagram for Jim Morrison.

Madonna once did a commercial for Pepsi.

Mick Jagger attended the London School of Economics for two years.

Paul McCartney's mother was a midwife.

Sheryl Crow's two front teeth are fake. She knocked them out when she tripped onstage earlier in her career.

ALSO KNOWN AS INTERMISSION

Breath, by Samuel Beckett, was first performed in April 1970. The play lasts thirty seconds and has no actors or dialogue.

DO NOT PASS GO

Since its introduction in February 1935, more than 250 million Monopoly board games have been sold worldwide.

Parker Brothers prints about $50 billion worth of Monopoly money in a year.

Every day, more money is printed for Monopoly than by the U.S. Treasury. The most money you can lose in one trip around the board (normal game rules, going to jail only once) is $26,040. The most money you can lose in one turn is $5,070.

Values on the Monopoly game board are the same today as they were in 1935.

The longest Monopoly game in a bathtub was ninety-nine hours long.

PLAY TO WIN

English gambling dens used to have employees whose job was to swallow the dice if the police arrived.

The word *checkmate* in chess comes from the Persian phrase *Shah-Mat*, which means "The king is dead."

According to Pope Innocent III, it was not a crime to kill someone after a game of chess.

Australia is considered the easiest continent to defend in the game Risk.

The Ouija board is named after the French and German words for "yes"—*oui* and *ja*.

Trivial Pursuit was invented by Canadians Scott Abbott and Chris Haney. They didn't want to pay the price for Scrabble, so they made up their own game.

Mario, of Super Mario Bros. fame, first appeared in the 1981 arcade game *Donkey Kong*. His original name was Jumpman, but that was changed to Mario to honor Nintendo of America, Inc.'s landlord, Mario Segali.

TV GUIDE

One in every four Americans has appeared on television.

Sitcom characters rarely say good-bye when they hang up the phone.

Daytime dramas are called soap operas because they were originally used to advertise soap powder. In America in the early days of television, advertisers would write stories around the use of their soap powder.

For many years, the globe on the NBC *Nightly News* spun in the wrong direction. On January 2, 1984, NBC finally set the world spinning in the proper direction.

Of the six men who made up The Three Stooges over the years, only three of them were real brothers.

There are as many as seventy-eight scenes in a single *X-Files* episode.

Gunsmoke was the top-rated series from 1957 to 1961.

The characters of Bert and Ernie on *Sesame Street* were named after Bert the cop and Ernie the taxi driver in Frank Capra's *It's a Wonderful Life*.

Every episode of *Seinfeld* contains a Superman reference somewhere.

❧ LIVE LONG AND PROSPER

Mr. Spock was second in command of the Starship *Enterprise*. His blood type was T-negative.

As well as appearing on *Star Trek*, William Shatner, Leonard Nimoy, James Doohan, and George Takei have all appeared at one time or another on *The Twilight Zone*.

The mask used by Michael Myers in the original *Halloween* movie was actually a Captain Kirk mask painted white.

Captain Jean-Luc Picard's fish was named Livingston.

Pokémon stands for "pocket monster."

Rocky Raccoon lives in the Black Hills of South Dakota.

The most common set of initials for Superman's friends and enemies is L.L.

☕ RETURN TO SENDER

The Simpsons live at 742 Evergreen Terrace, Springfield. The Munsters live at 1313 Mockingbird Lane, Mockingbird Heights. The Flintstones live at 39 Stone Canyon Way, Bedrock.

Scooby-Doo's real first name is Scoobert. Shaggy's real name is Norville. Casey Kasem was the voice of Shaggy.

☕ D'OH!

The Simpsons is the longest-running animated series on TV.

Matt Groening, creator of *The Simpsons*, incorporated his initials into the drawing of Homer. M is his hair, and G is his ear.

GOING 'NUTS

Peanuts is the world's most read comic strip.

Charlie Brown's father is a barber.

Lucy and Linus have another little brother named Rerun. He sometimes plays left field on Charlie Brown's baseball team—when he can find it!

EAT MORE SPINACH

Elzie Crisler Segar created the comic strip character Popeye in 1919.

> After the *Popeye* comic strip started in 1931, spinach consumption went up by 33 percent in the United States.

Popeye is five feet, six inches tall. He has an anchor tattooed on his arm.

> Popeye's adopted son is named Swee'pea.

LOONEY TUNES

Mel Blanc, who voiced Bugs Bunny, was allergic to carrots.

> Bugs Bunny first said "What's up, doc?" in the 1940 cartoon *A Wild Hare*.

The Looney Tunes theme song is actually called "The Merry-Go-Round Is Broken Down."

> Tweety used to be a baby bird without feathers until the censors decided he looked naked.

WHEN YOU WISH UPON A STAR

Walt Disney named Mickey Mouse after Mickey Rooney, whose mother he dated for some time. Walt Disney originally supplied the voice for Mickey Mouse.

Mickey Mouse is known as "Topolino" in Italy. He was the first nonhuman to win an Oscar. His birthday is November 18.

Mickey Mouse's ears are always turned to the front, no matter which direction his head is pointing.

Goofy has a wife, Mrs. Goofy, and one son, Goofy Jr.

Goofy actually started life as "Dippy Dawg," a combination of both Goofy and Pluto.

Donald Duck comics were banned in Finland because he doesn't wear pants.

Donald Duck's middle name is Fauntleroy. His sister is named Dumbella.

In *Fantasia*, the sorcerer's name is Yensid—*Disney* spelled backward.

Walt Disney's autograph bears no resemblance to the famous Disney logo.

CINEMA FIRSTS

The first real motion picture theater was called a nickelodeon—admission was a nickel—and opened in McKeesport, Pennsylvania, on June 19, 1905. The first motion picture shown there was *The Great Train Robbery*.

The first female monster to appear on the big screen was the Bride of Frankenstein.

The first James Bond movie was *Dr. No*.

The first word spoken by an ape in the movie *Planet of the Apes* is "Smile."

C3PO is the first character to speak in *Star Wars*.

Mrs. Claus's first name is Jessica in the movie *Santa Claus Is Coming to Town*.

WE ALL MAKE MISTAKES

During the chariot scene in *Ben-Hur*, a small red car can be seen in the distance.

In the film *Star Trek: First Contact*, when Picard shows Lilly she is orbiting Earth, Australia and Papua New Guinea are clearly visible . . . but New Zealand is missing.

If you pause *Saturday Night Fever* at the "How Deep Is Your Love" rehearsal scene, you will see the camera crew reflected in the dance hall mirror.

In 1976, Rodrigo's song "Guitar Concierto de Aranjuez" was number one in the United Kingdom for only three hours because of a computer error.

HOLLYWOOD INSIDER

When a film is in production, the last shot of the day is called the "martini shot"; the next-to-last one is called the "Abby Singer" after a famous assistant director.

Smithee is a pseudonym filmmakers use when they don't want their names to appear in the credits.

A "walla-walla" scene is one in which extras pretend to be talking in the background—when they say "walla-walla," it looks like they are actually having a conversation.

The Academy Award statue is named after a librarian's uncle. One day Margaret Herrick, librarian for the Academy of Motion Picture Arts and Sciences, made the remark that the statue looked like her uncle Oscar, and the name stuck.

In the early days of silent films, there was blatant thievery. Unscrupulous film companies would steal the film, reshoot a scene or two, and release it as a new production. To combat this, the Biograph Company put the company's trademark initials, AB, somewhere in every scene—on a door, a wall, or a window.

Ronald Reagan did a narration at the 1947 Academy Awards ceremony.

The second unit films movie shots that do not require the presence of actors.

Alfred Hitchcock never won an Academy Award for directing.

Because metal was scarce, the Academy Awards given out during World War II were made of wood.

A GALAXY FAR, FAR AWAY . . .

The actor who played Wedge in the original *Star Wars* trilogy has a famous nephew: actor Ewan McGregor, who plays young Obi-Wan in the new *Star Wars* trilogy.

Darth Vader is the only officer in the Imperial Forces who doesn't have a rank.

In the *Return of the Jedi* special edition, during the new Coruscant footage at the end of the film, a storm trooper can be seen being carried over the crowds.

Four people played Darth Vader: David Prowse was his body, James Earl Jones did the voice, Sebastian Shaw was his face, and a fourth person did his breathing.

Luke Skywalker's last name was changed at the last minute from Starkiller to make it less violent.

The name of Jabba the Hutt's pet spider monkey is Salacious Crumb.

YOU HAIRY APE

King Kong is the only movie to have its sequel (*Son of Kong*) released in the same year (1933).

Skull Island is the jungle home of King Kong.

ENJOY THE SHOW

Debra Winger was the voice of E.T.

Dirty Harry's last name is Callahan.

In Psycho, Mrs. Bates's dress was periwinkle blue.

SHAKEN, NOT STIRRED

Felix Leiter is James Bond's CIA contact.

James Bond is known as "Mr. Kiss-Kiss-Bang-Bang" in Italy.

Jean-Claude Van Damme was the alien in the original *Predator* in almost all the jumping and climbing scenes.

Godzilla has made the covers of *Time* and *Newsweek*.

Gone With the Wind is the only Civil War epic ever filmed without a single battle scene.

The movie *Clue* has three different endings. Each ending was randomly chosen for different theaters.

The movie *Paris, Texas* was banned in the city Paris, Texas, shortly after its box-office release.

The skyscraper in *Die Hard* is the Century Fox Tower.

The sound of E.T. walking was made by someone squishing her hands in jelly.

Dracula is the most filmed story of all time. *Dr. Jekyll and Mr. Hyde* is second, and *Oliver Twist* is third.

When the movie *The Wizard of Oz* first came out, it got bad reviews. The critics said it was stupid and uncreative.

THE NUMBERS GAME

Smokey the Bear's zip code is 20252.

Dirty Harry's badge number is 2211.

Sleeping Beauty slept one hundred years.

There are twenty-two stars surrounding the mountain on the Paramount Pictures logo.

In 1938, Joe Shuster and Jerry Siegel sold all rights to the comic-strip character *Superman* to their publishers for $130.

The number of the trash compactor in *Star Wars* is 3263827.

Pulp Fiction cost $8 million to make. Of that amount, $5 million went to actors' salaries.

In an episode of *The Simpsons*, Sideshow Bob's criminal number is 24601, the same as the criminal number of Jean Valjean in *Les Misérables*.

The longest film ever released was **** by Andy Warhol, which lasted twenty-four hours. It proved, not surprisingly (except perhaps to its creator), an utter failure. It was withdrawn and re-released in a ninety-minute form as *The Loves of Ondine*.

The longest Hollywood kiss was from the 1941 film *You're in the Army Now*; it lasted three minutes and three seconds.

A Chinese checkerboard has 121 holes.

There are 225 spaces on a Scrabble board.

There are one hundred squares on a Snakes and Ladders board.

The total number of bridge hands possible is 54 octillion.

There are 311,875,200 five-card hands possible in a fifty-two-card deck of cards.

The wheel on the game show *Wheel of Fortune* is 102 inches in diameter.

John Travolta's white suit from *Saturday Night Fever* was auctioned off for $145,500; Judy Garland's ruby slippers for $165,000; Charlie Chaplin's hat and cane for $211,500; Elvis's jacket for $59,700; and John Lennon's glasses for $25,875.

ALL THE CLASSICS

THE LITERARY WORLD

PAGE TO SCREEN

Bambi was originally published in 1929 in German.

General Lew Wallace's best-seller *Ben-Hur* was the first work of fiction to be blessed by a pope.

The name for Oz in *The Wizard of Oz* was thought up when the author, L. Frank Baum, looked at his filing cabinet and saw A–N and O–Z, hence Oz.

THE USELESS INFORMATION BOOK CLUB

An estimated 2.5 million books will be shipped in the next twelve months with the wrong covers.

Susan Haswell Rowson was America's first bestselling novelist for her novel *Charlotte Goode*.

Mick Jagger turned down a £3.5 million advance offer on his memoirs from a publisher because, he said, he "couldn't remember" enough significant details from his own life.

According to Ernest Hemingway, four achievements are necessary to become a real man. You should plant a tree, fight a bull, write a book, and have a son.

A woman who returned a book in a very tattered state to the Stroud Library in Gloucestershire, England, explained it was the fault of her dog, which had chewed it. The name of the book was *How to Train Your Dog*.

During his entire lifetime, Herman Melville's timeless classic of the sea, *Moby Dick*, only sold fifty copies.

Lassie, the TV collie, first appeared in a 1930s short novel titled *Lassie Come Home*, written by Eric Mowbray Knight. The dog in the novel was based on Knight's real-life collie, Toots.

In Africa the house of the wicked witch in *Hansel and Gretel* is not made of gingerbread but of salt—which was highly prized by children.

In Victorian times Goldilocks, of Three Bears fame, was known as Silver Hair. She later became Golden Hair and eventually Goldilocks.

In 1898 (fourteen years prior to the *Titanic* tragedy), Morgan Robertson wrote a novel called *Futility*. The plot of the novel turned on the largest ship ever built hitting an iceberg in the Atlantic Ocean on a cold April night.

Keeping Warm with an Axe is the title of a real how-to book.

Mary Shelley wrote *Frankenstein* at the age of nineteen.

Virginia Woolf wrote all her books standing up.

At twelve years old, an African man named Ernest Loftus made his first entry in his diary and continued every day for ninety-one years.

The only person to decline a Pulitzer Prize for Fiction was Sinclair Lewis for his book *Arrowsmith*.

Roger Ebert is the only film critic to have ever won the Pulitzer Prize.

Samuel Clemens, aka Mark Twain, smoked forty cigars a day for the last years of his life. He was born in 1835 when Halley's Comet appeared. He died in 1910 when Halley's Comet returned.

Ghosts appear in four Shakespearian plays: *Julius Caesar*, *Richard III*, *Hamlet*, and *Macbeth*.

World heavyweight boxing champion Gene Tunney also lectured on Shakespeare at Yale University later in his life.

Shakespeare spelled his own name several different ways.

Goethe couldn't stand the sound of barking dogs and could only write if he had an apple rotting in the drawer of his desk.

Ernest Vincent Wright wrote the fifty-thousand-word novel *Gatsby* without any word containing "e."

Dr. Seuss coined the word *nerd* in his 1950 book *If I Ran the Zoo*.

Sherlock Holmes's archenemy was Professor Moriarty. Holmes had a smarter brother named Mycroft.

Sherlock Holmes never said, "Elementary, my dear Watson."

Isaac Asimov is the only author to have a book in every Dewey decimal category.

Jacqueline Kennedy Onassis was the most famous editor at Doubleday & Co.

Hans Christian Anderson, author of many famous fairy tales, was word-blind. He never learned to spell correctly, and his publishers always found errors in his manuscripts.

Dr. Jekyll's first name is Henry.

Charles Dickens never finished his schooling. He was also an insomniac, who believed his best chance of sleeping was in the center of a bed facing directly north.

BIBLE TALK

Almost all the villains in the Bible have red hair.

The longest chapter in the Bible is Psalms 119.

There are more than 1,700 references to gems and precious stones in the King James Version of the Bible.

The book of Esther in the Bible is the only book that does not mention the name of God.

The term *devil's advocate* comes from the Roman Catholic Church. When deciding if someone should be sainted, a devil's advocate is always appointed to give an alternative view.

The Bible has been translated into Klingon.

It is believed that Shakespeare was forty-six around the time the King James Version of the Bible was written. In Psalms 46, the forty-sixth word from the first word is *shake*, and the forty-sixth word from the last word is *spear*.

Every minute, forty-seven Bibles are sold or distributed throughout the world.

According to Genesis 1:20–22, the chicken came before the egg.

> All Hebrew-originating names that end with the letters "el" have something to do with God.

A seventeenth-century Swedish philologist claimed that in the Garden of Eden God spoke Swedish, Adam spoke Danish, and the serpent spoke French.

ARE YOU AFRAID OF THE DARK?

A phonophobe fears noise.

> Nyctohylophobia is the fear of dark wooded areas, or forests at night.

Pyrophobia is the fear of fire.

> Taphephobia is the fear of being buried alive.

Papaphobia is the fear of popes.

> Nycrophobia is the fear of darkness.

Lachanophobia is the fear of vegetables.

Entomophobia is the fear of insects.

Eosophobia is the fear of dawn.

Arnold Schonberg suffered from triskaidecphobia, the fear of the number thirteen. He died thirteen minutes from midnight on Friday the thirteenth.

Zoophobia is the fear of animals.

Xenophobia is the fear of strangers or foreigners.

Phobatrivaphobia is fear of trivia about phobias.

NOW SAY IT THREE TIMES FAST

A hydrodaktulpsychicharmonica is a variety of musical glass.

Hydroxydesoxycorticosterone and hydroxydeoxycorticosterones are the longest anagrams.

The letters KGB stand for Komitet Gosudarstvennoy Bezopasnos.

The longest place name in Great Britain is that of a Welsh village: Gorsafawddachaidraigddanheddogled-dollonpenrhynareurdraethceredigion.

IN THE BEGINNING

During early years of feudal rule in England, each shire had a reeve who was the law for that shire, called the shire reeve. When the term was taken to America, it was shortened to sheriff.

The phrase "sleep tight" originated when mattresses were set upon ropes woven through the bed frame. To remedy sagging ropes, one would use a bed key to tighten the rope.

The word robot comes from the Czechoslovakian word *robotovat*, which means "to work very hard." It was created by Karel Capek.

The word *noon* came from an old church term *none*, meaning "three." There was a monastic order that was so devout they declared they would not eat until that time. Because they rang the bells indicating time, "none" came earlier and earlier. The townspeople called midday noon to ridicule them.

Before the turn of the century, newspapers were called tabloids, chronicles, gazettes, etc. Most had local stories, and far away stories were quite old because it took a while for stories to travel (and of course, they were subject to changes from hand to hand). With the advent of the teletype, stories could be broadcast all over at unheard-of speed. Several of the papers started carrying a section with stories from all over—north, east, west, and south—and that's why they are called *news*papers.

Some coins used in the American colonies before the Revolutionary War were Spanish dollars, which could be cut into pieces, or bits. Because two pieces equaled one-quarter dollar, the expression "two bits" came into being as a name for twenty-five cents.

Ham radio operators coined the word *ham* from the expression "ham-fisted operators," a term used to describe early radio users who sent Morse code by pounding their fists.

"Happy as a clam" is from the expression "happy as a clam at high tide." Clams are only harvested when the tide is out.

The difference between a nook and a cranny is that the nook is a corner and the cranny is a crack.

The grand jury used to write *ignoramus* on the backs of indictments not found or not to be sent to court. This was often misconstrued as an indication of the stupidity of the jury, hence its present meaning.

The State Department refers to elevators as "vertical transportation units."

In the late nineteenth century and earlier years of the twentieth century, when gramophones or phonographs amplified the sound through large horns, woolen socks were often stuffed in them to cut down the noise; hence the phrase "put a sock in it."

The phrase "Often a bridesmaid, but never a bride" actually comes from an advertisement for Listerine mouthwash.

The term *honeymoon* is derived from the Babylonians, who declared mead, a honey-flavored wine, the official wedding drink, stipulating that the bride's parents be required to keep the groom supplied with the drink for the month following the wedding.

The phrase "the boogeyman will get you" refers to the Boogey people who still inhabit an area of Indonesia. These people still act as pirates today and attack passing ships.

The term *mayday* used for signaling for help (after SOS) comes from the French *M'aidez*, which is pronounced *mayday* and means "help me."

"Three-dog night" (attributed to Australian Aborigines) came about because on especially cold nights, these nomadic people needed three dogs around them to keep from freezing.

In 1943, Navy officer Grace Hopper found a glitch in her computer. After investigating, she discovered the system had a bug—a real one. It turned out a moth had made its way into Hopper's computer. Though the word *bug* has meant "fault" or "defect" since as far back as the 1870s, Hopper's story is credited with making it the synonym of choice in the computer industry.

According to the *Encyclopedia Britannica, 11th Edition*, from 1910–1911, the word *toast* was borrowed from the Old French *toste*, which has the Latin root of *torrere, tostum*, meaning "to scorch or burn."

The letters of the word SHAZAM, which was shouted to conjure up comic-book hero Captain Marvel, stood for Solomon's Wisdom, Hercules's Strength, Atlas's Stamina, Zeus's Power, Achilles's Courage, and Mercury's Speed.

FOREIGN TRANSLATION

German is considered the sister language of English.

Amphibious is based on Greek words that mean living a double life; amphibians live both on land and in water.

The word *rodent* comes from the Latin word *rodere*, meaning "to gnaw."

The words *assassination* and *bump* were invented by Shakespeare.

American billion is one thousand million—a British billion is one million million.

The Old English word for sneeze is *fneosam*.

The *U* in U-boats stands for "underwater."

The word *constipation* comes from a Latin word that means "to crowd together."

In most of the world's languages the word for mother begins with the letter *m*.

seven-letter word that contains ten other words without any of the letters being rearranged is *therein*. It includes *the, there, he, in, rein, her, here, ere, therein,* and *herein*.

The only word in the English language that both begins and ends with the letters *und* is *underground*.

The most commonly used word in English conversation is *I*.

The word *curfew* originates from an old French word that means "cover fire."

Corduroy comes from the French *cord du roi* or "cloth of the king."

In French, *essay* means "to try, attempt."

The word *accordion* comes from the German word *akkord*, which means "agreement, harmony."

The shortest French word with all five vowels is *oiseau*, meaning bird.

In ancient Greece, writing had no space between the words.

Left-handed people cannot write Mandarin Chinese.

Dreamt is the only English word that ends in the letters *mt*.

The word *calendar* comes from Latin and means "to call out."

The word *hangnail* comes from the Middle English: *ang-* ("painful") + *nail*. It has nothing to do with hanging.

The word *kangaroo* means "I don't know" in the language of Australian Aborigines. When Captain Cook approached natives of the Endeavor River tribe to ask what the strange animal he spotted was, he got "kangaroo" for an answer.

The word *cop* came from the English term "Constable on Patrol."

IN CASE YOU WERE WONDERING

A prestidigitator is another word for magician.

A conchologist studies mollusks and shells.

A fingerprint is also known as a dactylogram.

A klazomaniac is someone who feels like shouting.

A librocubicularist is someone who reads in bed.

A phrenologist feels and interprets skull features.

A sultan's wife is called a sultana.

Spat-out food is called chanking.

The ball on top of a flagpole is called the truck.

The word *lethologica* describes the state of not remembering the word you want to say.

The word *samba* means to rub navels together.

When your sink is full, the little hole that lets the water drain, instead of flowing over the side, is called a porcelator.

Women who wink at men are known as nictitating women.

A poem written to celebrate a wedding is called an epithalamium.

According to author Douglas Adams, a salween is the faint taste of dishwashing liquid in a cup of fresh tea.

Alma mater means "bountiful mother."

An animal epidemic is called an epizootic.

The Japanese word *judo* means "the gentle way."

The Australian slang term *hooloo* means "good-bye."

The word *monosyllable* has five syllables.

A *vexillologist* studies flags.

Degringolade means "to fall and disintegrate."

Dendrology is the study of trees.

A *trilemma* is a dilemma with a third alternative.

Dibble means "to drink like a duck."

EEG stands for electroencephalogram.

Groaking is to watch people eating in the hope that they will offer you some.

Karaoke means "empty orchestra" in Japanese.

Kemosabe means "soggy shrub" in Navajo.

Koala is Aboriginal for "no drink."

Lead poisoning is known as plumbism.

Scatologists are experts who study feces.

The "You Are Here" arrow on a map is called the IDEO locator.

The third year of marriage is the leather anniversary.

The original meaning of the word clue was a ball of thread or yarn. Like its modern namesake, it often took some time to unravel.

The abbreviation "e.g." stands for "*exempli gratia,*" or "for example."

The abbreviation for pound, "lb.," comes from the astrological sign Libra, meaning "balance."

The French term *bourrage de crane* for wartime propaganda means "brain stuffing."

The infinity character on the keyboard is called a lemniscate.

The Japanese translation of *switch* is pronounced *suitchi.*

The name for fungal remains found in coal is sclerotinite.

The phrase "jet lag" was once called boat lag, back before airplanes existed.

The Sanskrit word for war means "desire for more cows."

The slash character is called a virgule, or solidus.

The word *byte* is a contraction of "by eight."

Trabant is the German word for "satellite."

Zorro means "fox" in Spanish.

A group of officers is called a mess.

The next-to-last event is the penultimate, and the second-to-last is the antepenultimate.

The highest-scoring three-letter word in Scrabble is zax, which is a tool for cutting and trimming roof slates.

The symbol on the pound key is called an anoctothorpe.

SEMANTICS

Naked means "to be unprotected"; *nude* means "unclothed."

A hamlet is a village without a church, and a town is not a city until it has a cathedral.

FUN WITH LETTERS

Of all the words in the English language, the word *set* has the most definitions.

Rhythm and *syzygy* are the longest English words without vowels.

Skepticisms is the longest typed word that alternates hands.

The letter *J* does not appear anywhere on the periodic table of elements.

The only fifteen-letter word that can be spelled without repeating a letter is *uncopyrightable*.

The only contemporary words that end with -*gry* are *angry* and *hungry*.

Only four words in the English language end in -*dous*: *tremendous*, *horrendous*, *stupendous*, and *hazardous*.

Only three world capitals begin with the letter *O* in English: Ottawa, Canada; Oslo, Norway; and Ouagadougou, Burkina Faso.

Six words in the English language have the letter combination *uu*: muumuu, vacuum, continuum, duumvirate, duumvir, and residuum.

Ten body parts are only three letters long: eye, ear, leg, arm, jaw, gum, toe, lip, hip, and rib.

There was no punctuation until the fifteenth century.

You would have to count to one thousand to use the letter *A* in the English language to spell a whole number.

Facetious and *abstemious* contain all the vowels in the correct order, as does *arsenious*, meaning "containing arsenic."

Cleveland spelled backward is *DNA level C*.

Hawaiian words do not contain consonant clusters. For example, Kahlúa is not a Hawaiian word.

"I am" is the shortest complete sentence in the English language.

In English, four is the only number that has the same number of letters as its value.

Stewardesses is the longest word that is typed with only the left hand.

No word in the English language rhymes with month, orange, silver, or purple.

Quisling is the only word in the English language to start with "quis."

Maine is the only state whose name is just one syllable.

The most recent year that could be written upside down and right side up and appear the same was 1961. The next year this will be possible will be 6009.

LANGUAGE BARRIER

Chevrolet tried marketing a Chevrolet Nova in Spanish-speaking countries—it didn't sell well because *"no va"* means "doesn't go" in Spanish.

In Italy, a campaign for Schweppes Tonic Water translated the name into Schweppes Toilet Water.

In Papua New Guinea, there are villages within five miles of each other that speak different languages.

More than twenty-six dialects of Quichua are spoken in Ecuador.

Native speakers of Japanese learn Spanish more easily than English. Native speakers of English learn Spanish more easily than Japanese.

Polish is the only word in the English language that, when capitalized, is changed from a noun or a verb to a nationality.

Rio de Janeiro translates to River of January.

The correct response to the Irish greeting "Top of the morning to you" is, "And the rest of the day to yourself."

The *D* in D-day stands for "day." The French term for D-day is *J-jour*.

The stress in Hungarian words always falls on the first syllable.

The Eskimo language has more than twenty words to describe different kinds of snow.

WAS IT AT CHUCK E. CHEESE?

The earliest document in Latin in a woman's handwriting is an invitation to a birthday party from the first century C.E.

SPECIAL OCCASIONS

World Tourist Day is observed on September 27.

October 10 is National Metric Day.

November 29 is National Sinky Day, a day to eat over one's sink and worship it.

COMMON THREADS

The most common name in the world is Mohammed.

The most common Spanish surname is Garcia.

The most common Russian surname is Ivanov.

The most common Swedish surname is Johansson.

ALL THE GREATS

Each of the sunflowers in Vincent Van Gogh's painting *Sunflowers,* which sold at auction in 1987, was worth $2.66 million. There are fifteen in the painting.

The sitter in Leonardo da Vinci's *Mona Lisa* has no eyebrows.

When asked to name his favorite among all his paintings, Pablo Picasso replied, "the next one."

Mark Twain failed to graduate from elementary school.

Only two of the Sherlock Holmes stories are written with him as the narrator. They are *The Blanched Soldier* and *The Lion's Mane.*

Dr. Frankenstein's first name was Victor.

Robin Hood's friend Little John was really named John Little.

In the Batman stories the Riddler's real name was Edward Nigma or E. Nigma.

Half the world's population has seen at least one James Bond movie.

ON THE MENU

WATER WORLD

Drinking water after eating reduces the acid in your mouth by 61 percent.

Forty-eight million people in the United States receive their drinking water from private or household wells.

In the typical Canadian home, 45 percent of water is used for the toilet, 28 percent is used for bathing and personal matters, 23 percent is used for laundry or dishes, and 4 percent is used for cooking or drinking purposes.

It's impossible to get water out of a rimless tire.

Less than 2 percent of the water on Earth is fresh.

THE HOUSE THAT RONALD BUILT

Ray Kroc bought McDonald's for $2.7 million in 1961 from the McDonald brothers.

> A man named Ed Peterson is the inventor of the Egg McMuffin.

The big *M* on McDonald's signs in Paris is the only one in the world that is white, rather than yellow; it was thought that yellow was too tacky.

> McDonald's in New Zealand serves apricot pies instead of cherry ones.

The McDonald's at The Skydome in Toronto is the only one in the world that sells hot dogs.

> On average, there are 178 sesame seeds on each McDonald's Big Mac bun.

SODA OR POP?

Carbonated water, with nothing else in it, can dissolve limestone, talc, and many other low-Mohs hardness minerals. Coincidentally, carbonated water is the main ingredient in soda pop.

The citrus soda 7-Up was created in 1929; "7" was selected because the original containers were seven ounces. "Up" indicated the direction of the bubbles.

Fanta Orange is the third largest selling soft drink in the world.

Coca-Cola was first served at Jacob's Pharmacy in Atlanta in 1886 for only five cents a glass. The formula for Coca-Cola was created by pharmacist John Pemberton. Only two people in the world know the secret recipe for Coca-Cola.

Earl Dean developed the bottle design for Coca-Cola.

Pepsi originally contained pepsin, hence the name.

The first western consumer product sold in the former Soviet Union was Pepsi Cola.

989, Pepsi came out with a morning soft drink called Pepsi AM. It didn't last long on the market.

Pepsi is commonly used by wooden boat owners to clean mold from decks. You can spill it on for about thirty seconds, but it needs to be rinsed to be sure it does not erode the decks completely.

HOLD YOUR LIQUOR

A full 7 percent of the entire Irish barley crop goes to the production of Guinness beer.

Beer foam will go down if you lick your finger and then stick it in the beer.

Researchers in Denmark found that beer tastes best when drunk to the accompaniment of a certain musical tone. The optimal frequency is different for each beer, they reported. The correct harmonious tone for Carlsberg lager, for example, is 510 to 520 cycles per second.

The Bloody Mary is known as the "Queen of Drinks" and was invented in Harry's Bar in Paris in the 1930s.

If you put a raisin in a glass of champagne, it will keep floating to the top and sinking to the bottom.

The first man to distill bourbon whiskey was a Baptist preacher in 1789.

In Japan, Christmas Eve is a time to eat strawberry short-cake and fried chicken.

Tic Tacs contain carnauba wax—the same ingredient found in many car polishes.

More cat food is bought in Britain each year than can be eaten by the number of cats in the country.

You cannot taste food unless it is mixed with saliva. This is true for all foods.

Sarsaparilla is the root that flavors root beer.

French fries were invented in Belgium.

The herring is the most widely eaten fish in the world.

Dr. Miles's compound extract of tomato—an early ketchup—was sold as a medicine in the nineteenth century.

Black-eyed peas are beans.

Ancient Egyptians would place their right hands on onions when swearing an oath. Its round shape symbolized eternity.

Wine will spoil if exposed to light, hence the tinted bottles.

Lab tests can detect traces of alcohol in urine six to twelve hours after a person has stopped drinking.

In medieval England, beer was often served with breakfast.

CRACKING SOME NUTS

Almonds are a member of the peach family. They are the oldest, most widely cultivated and extensively used nuts in the world.

Peanuts are cholesterol-free. They are one of the ingredients of dynamite.

George Washington Carver invented peanut butter. It takes more than five hundred peanuts to make one twelve-ounce jar of peanut butter.

Australian chemist John Macadamia discovered the macadamia nut.

The only real food U.S. astronauts are allowed in space are pecan nuts.

EAT YOUR VEGGIES

Ninety percent of the vitamin C in brussels sprouts is lost in cooking.

You use more calories eating celery than there are in celery itself.

Eggplant is a member of the thistle family.

Onions are low in calories and a good source of vitamin C, calcium, potassium, and fiber. They also help circulation.

Onions get their distinctive smell by soaking up sulfur from the soil.

The oldest known vegetable is the pea.

The most popular sweet pepper is the bell pepper.

The heat of peppers is rated on the Scoville scale.

The color of a chili is no indication of its spiciness, but size usually is—the smaller the pepper, the hotter it is.

Pumpkins contain vitamin A and potassium.

TUTTI FRUITY

Apples, not caffeine, are more efficient for waking you up in the morning.

You can make a glass of apple cider with only three apples.

The pineapple originated in South America and did not reach Hawaii until the early nineteenth century.

There are no bananas in banana oil.

The largest fruit crop on earth is grapes—followed by bananas.

Fresh apples float because 25 percent of their volume is air.

The avocado has the most calories of any fruit.

The average banana weighs 4 ounces.

Approximately seventeen thousand bananas are eaten each week in the Boston University dining room.

Bananas do not grow on trees but on rhizomes.

Cranberry jelly is the only jelly flavor that comes from the real fruit, not artificial flavoring.

Lemons contain more sugar than strawberries.

Seeds are missing from a navel orange. The bigger the navel, the sweeter the orange.

In Ivrea, Italy, thousands of citizens celebrate the beginning of Lent by throwing oranges at one another.

Orange juice helps the body absorb iron easily when consumed with a meal.

The most common pear worldwide is the Bartlett. It is bell shaped, sweet, and soft, with a light green color.

Pineapples do not ripen after they have been picked.

Tomatina is the legendary Spanish tomato-throwing festival.

More than two hundred varieties of watermelon are grown in the United States.

JAVA TIME

Coffee is the world's most popular stimulant. It is the second largest item of international commerce in the world.

When a coffee seed is planted, it takes five years to yield consumable fruit.

There are more than one hundred chemicals in one cup of coffee.

Too much caffeine can cause heart palpitations.

A Saudi Arabian woman can get a divorce if her husband doesn't give her coffee.

YOU SAY TOMATO, I SAY AVOCADO

A chili pepper isn't a pepper. In fact, more than two hundred kinds of chili peppers aren't peppers.

The peanut is a vegetable and a member of the pea family.

THE SWEET SPOT

M&Ms stands for the last names of Forrest Mars Sr., the sweet maker, and his associate, Bruce Murrie. The candy was developed so soldiers could eat sweets without getting their fingers sticky.

The top layer of a wedding cake, known as the groom's cake, is usually a fruit cake so it will last until the couple's first anniversary, when they often eat it.

As much as fifty gallons of maple sap are used to make a single gallon of maple sugar.

Pound cake is so called because the original recipe required one pound of butter.

Honey is used as a center for golf balls and in antifreeze mixtures.

When honey is swallowed, it enters the blood stream within a period of twenty minutes.

Ice cream was originally made without sugar and eggs. Seaweed is one of the ingredients in some ice cream.

Less than 3 percent of Nestlé's sales are for chocolate.

Eleanor Roosevelt ate three chocolate-covered garlic balls every day for most of her adult life.

Eating chocolate was once considered a temptation of the devil.

NO WONDER WE'RE FAT

A can of SPAM is opened every four seconds.

The word spam is an acronym formed from SPiced hAM.

Americans on average eat eighteen acres of pizza every day.

GREAT MOMENTS IN GASTRONOMIC HISTORY

The food of the Greek gods was called ambrosia.

Blueberry Jelly Bellies were created especially for Ronald Reagan.

California's Frank Epperson invented the Popsicle in 1905, when he was eleven years old.

Chefs started using onions five thousand years ago to spice up their cooking.

Dry cereal for breakfast was invented by John Henry Kellogg at the turn of the twentieth century.

Fortune cookies were actually invented in America by Charles Jung in 1918.

Miss Piggy once said, "Never eat more than you can lift."

Jelly Belly jelly beans were the first jelly beans in outer space when they went up with astronauts in the June 21, 1983, voyage of the space shuttle *Challenger*.

The ancient Romans often paid their taxes in honey.

Laws forbidding the sale of sodas on Sunday prompted William Garwood to invent the ice-cream sundae in Evanston, Illinois, in 1875.

Potatoes were first imported by Europe in the 1500s on Spanish ships returning from Peru.

The English word *soup* comes from the Middle Ages word *sop*, which means a slice of bread over which roast drippings were poured.

COUNTERINTUITIVE BUT TRUE

Vanilla is used to make chocolate.

RECORD BREAKERS

The highest lifetime yield of milk for a single cow is 55,849 gallons.

The hottest chili in the world is the habanero.

The largest hamburger in the world weighed in at 5,520 pounds.

INTERNATIONAL PALATES

Dinner guests during the medieval times in England were expected to bring their own knives to the table.

In eighteenth-century France, visitors to the royal palace in Versailles were allowed to stand in a roped-off section of the main dining room and watch the king and queen eat.

In certain parts of India and ancient China, mouse meat was considered a delicacy.

Each year, Americans spend more on cat food than on baby food.

Due to turkey's high sulfur content, Americans also produce enough gas to fly a fleet of seventy-five *Hindenburgs* from Los Angeles to New York in twenty-four hours.

> The Southern dish "chitlins" is made up of pigs' small intestines.

The world's number-one producer and consumer of fresh pork is China.

> China produces 278,564,356,980 eggs per year.

China's Beijing Duck Restaurant can seat nine thousand people at one time.

> If China imported just 10 percent of its rice needs, the price on the world market would increase by 80 percent.

More than half of the different types of cheese in the world come from France.

> The glue on Israeli postage stamps is certified kosher.

Japan is the largest exporter of frogs' legs.

> A company in Taiwan makes dinnerware out of wheat, so you can eat your plate.

CULINARY ER

Since 1978, at least thirty-seven people have died as a result of shaking vending machines in an attempt to get free merchandise. More than one hundred have been injured.

Some people drink the urine of pregnant women to build up their immune systems.

The liquid inside young coconuts can be used as a substitute for blood plasma in an emergency.

You should not eat a crayfish with a straight tail. It was dead before it was cooked.

Nutmeg is extremely poisonous if injected intravenously.

A LITTLE BIT GRAINY

There are more than fifteen thousand different kinds of rice. Rice is grown on more than 10 percent of the earth's farmable surface and is the main food for half of the people of the world.

Rice is thrown at weddings as a symbol of fertility.

Shredded Wheat was the first ready-to-eat breakfast cereal.

The wheat that produces a one-pound loaf of bread requires two tons of water to grow.

SO THAT'S WHERE OUR
TAX DOLLARS GO

The U.S. government spent $277,000 on "pickle research" in 1993.

FEELING SAUCY

Only 5 percent of salt produced ends up on the dinner table. The rest is used for packing meat; building roads; feeding livestock; tanning leather; and manufacturing glass, soap, ash, and washing compounds.

Salt is one of the few spices that is all taste and no smell.

Table salt is the only commodity that hasn't risen dramatically in price in the last one hundred fifty years.

Tabasco sauce is made by fermenting vinegar and hot peppers in a French oak barrel that has three inches of salt on top and is aged for three years until all the salt is diffused through the barrel.

Worcestershire sauce is basically anchovy ketchup.

The number 57 on a Heinz ketchup bottle represents the number of varieties of pickle the company once had.

THINGS THAT MAKE YOU GO "MOOO . . ."

Reindeer's milk has more fat than cow's milk.

Sheep's milk is used to produce Roquefort cheese.

The fat molecules in goat's milk are five times smaller than those found in cow's milk.

In Hong Kong soy milk is as popular as Coca-Cola is in the West.

Cream does not weigh as much as milk.

More people are allergic to cow's milk than to any other food.

Eighty-seven percent of fully fat milk is water.

AROUND THE HOUSE

DEUCES ARE WILD

Each king in a deck of playing cards represents a great king from history: spades—King David, clubs—Alexander the Great, hearts—Charlemagne, and diamonds—Julius Caesar.

Each of the suits in a deck of cards represents the four major pillars of the economy in the Middle Ages: hearts represented the Church, spades represented the military, clubs represented agriculture, and diamonds represented the merchant class.

For a deck of cards to be mixed up enough to play with properly, it should be shuffled at least seven times.

Playing cards became the first paper currency of Canada in 1685, when the French governor used them to pay off some war debts.

Playing cards in India are round.

The Nine of Hearts playing card is considered the symbol of love.

COMMON CENTS

The ridges on the sides of coins are called reeding or milling. A dime has 118 ridges around the edge. A quarter has 119 ridges.

How valuable is the penny you found lying on the ground? If it takes just a second to pick it up, a person could make $36 per hour just picking up pennies.

On the new U.S. $100 bill, the time on the clock tower of Independence Hall is 4:10.

The Australian $5, $10, $20, $50, and $100 notes are made of plastic.

The face of a penny can hold thirty drops of water.

The first coins issued by authority of the United States government were minted in 1787. These pennies were inscribed with the plainspoken motto, "Mind your own business."

The original fifty-cent piece in Australian decimal currency had around $100 worth of silver in it before it was replaced with a less-expensive twelve-sided coin.

At the height of inflation in Germany in the early 1920s, approximately two dollars were equal to a quintillion German marks.

KISSABLY FRESH

More people use blue toothbrushes than red ones.

Oral-B is a combination of "oral hygiene" and the letter B, which stands for the word *better*.

Some toothpaste contains antifreeze.

Dentists recommended that a toothbrush be kept six feet away from a toilet to avoid airborne particles resulting from the flush.

Americans spend $1.5 billion every year on toothpaste.

JUST A SCRATCH

Four thousand people are injured by teapots every year.

Every year, more than 8,800 people injure themselves in some way with a toothpick.

On average, one hundred people choke on ballpoint pens every year.

Forty thousand Americans are injured by toilets every year.

Each year, there are about fifteen thousand vacuum cleaner–related accidents in the United States.

THE ROYAL THRONE

A flush toilet exists today that dates back to 2000 B.C.E.

About a third of people flush while they are still sitting on the toilet.

Alaska has more outhouses than any other state.

In 1825, the first toilet was installed in the White House.

Most toilets flush in E flat.

Poet Henry Wadsworth Longfellow was the first American to have plumbing installed in his house, in 1840.

The first toilet ever seen on television was on *Leave It to Beaver*.

The Soviet Sukhoi-34 is the first strike fighter with a toilet in it.

Toilets in Australia flush counterclockwise.

SIMPLY SARTORIAL

Bill Bowerman, founder of Nike, got his first shoe idea after staring at a waffle iron. He got the idea of using squared spikes to make shoes lighter.

The plastic things on the end of shoelaces are called aglets.

If you lace your shoes from the inside to the outside, the fit will be snugger around your big toe.

Jeans were named after Genoa, Italy, where the first denim cloth was made.

The YKK on the zipper of your jeans stands for Yoshida Kogyo Kabushibibaisha, the world's largest zipper manufacturer.

Neckties were first worn in Croatia. That's why they were called cravats (*cro-vats*).

Most people button their shirts upward.

The armhole in clothing is called an armsaye.

TOYING AROUND

On average there are 62 LEGO bricks for every person on earth.

Ninety-four percent of all households in Belgium with children under the age of fourteen years old own Lego products.

Barbie's full name is Barbara Millicent Roberts.

There are more Barbie dolls in Italy than there are Canadians in Canada.

Slinkys were invented by an airplane mechanic; he was playing with engine parts and realized the possible secondary use of one of the springs.

The Slinky is sold on every continent of the world except Antarctica. If you took a standard Slinky and stretched it out, it would measure eighty-seven feet.

In 1946, the first TV toy commercial aired. It was for Mr. Potato Head.

It takes an average of 48 to 100 tries to solve a Rubik's Cube puzzle. If done perfectly, any Rubik's Cube combination can be solved in seventeen turns.

The hula hoop was the biggest-selling toy in 1957.

The yo-yo originated in the Philippines, where it is used as a weapon in hunting.

The hundred billionth crayon made by Crayola was Periwinkle Blue.

In the 1985 Boise, Idaho, mayoral election, there were four write-in votes for Mr. Potato Head.

WHAT DO YOU MEAN?

Camera shutter speed B stands for "bulb."

Mosquito repellants do not repel. They hide you. The spray blocks the mosquito's sensors so they do not know you are there.

Scotchgard is a combination of the words *Scotch*, meaning "Scotsman," and a misspelling of *guard*, meaning "to protect."

The holes in flyswatters are used to lower air resistance.

Scotch tape has been used as an anti-corrosive shield on the *Goodyear Blimp*.

HAMMER TIME

The side of a hammer is called a cheek.

The end of a hammer, opposite the striking end, is called a peen.

THE IVORY TOWER

Ivory bar soap floating was the result of a mistake. The manufacturer had been mixing the soap formula and causing excess air bubbles that made it float. Customers wrote and told them how much they loved that it floated, and it has floated ever since.

FEELING A BIT AVERAGE

The average person looks at eight houses before buying one.

The average lead pencil can draw a line thirty-five miles long or write approximately fifty thousand English words.

The average woman consumes six pounds of lipstick in her lifetime.

ALTERNATIVE FUNCTIONS

Ketchup is excellent for cleaning brass, especially tarnished or corroded brass.

Kleenex tissues were originally used as filters in gas masks.

Mixing Sani-Flush and Comet cleaners has been known to cause explosions.

DISHING THE DIRT

Each of us generates five pounds of garbage a day; most of it is paper.

It takes a plastic container fifty thousand years to start decomposing.

According to a market research survey, 68 percent of consumers who receive junk mail actually open the envelopes.

MEASURING UP

The diameter of the wire in a standard paper clip is 1 millimeter, or about 0.04 inches.

Aluminum is strong enough to support ninety thousand pounds per square inch.

KEEPING YOUR COOL

Rubber bands last longer when refrigerated.

Some Eskimos have been known to use refrigerators to keep their food from freezing.

HOME DÉCOR

A good-quality Persian rug, which contains one million knots in every three square inches, can last as long as five hundred years.

A typical double mattress contains as many as two million house dust mites.

HISTORY'S MYSTERIES

HOW DO YOU PLEAD?

A Virginia law requires all bathtubs to be kept out in the yard, not inside the house.

Celebrating Christmas was once illegal in England.

Dueling is legal in Paraguay as long as both parties are registered blood donors.

In a tradition dating back to the beginning of the Westminster system of government, the bench in the middle of a Westminster parliament is two-and-a-half sword lengths long. This was so the government and opposition couldn't have a go at each other if it all got a bit heated.

In Alaska, it is illegal to shoot at a moose from the window of an airplane or other flying vehicle.

In Athens, Greece, a driver's license can be taken away by law if the driver is deemed either "unbathed" or "poorly dressed."

In Baltimore, it is illegal to wash or scrub a sink, regardless of how dirty it is.

In Cleveland, Ohio, it is illegal to catch mice without a hunting license.

In Hartford, Connecticut, it is illegal for a husband to kiss his wife on Sundays.

In Helsinki, Finland, instead of giving parking tickets, the police usually deflate tires.

In Jasmine, Saskatchewan, it is illegal for a cow to moo within three hundred kilometers of a private home.

In Kentucky, it is illegal to carry ice cream in your back pocket.

In Texas, it is illegal to put graffiti on someone else's cow.

It is against the law to stare at the mayor of Paris.

In Sweden, it is illegal to train a seal to balance a ball on its nose.

In California, it is illegal to eat oranges while bathing.

In Bladworth, Saskatchewan, it is illegal to frown at cows.

In Arizona, it is illegal to hunt camels.

In Malaysia, it is illegal for restaurants to substitute toilet paper as table napkins. Repeat offenders go to jail.

It used to be law in France that children's names had to be taken from an official government list.

In Iceland, it was once against the law to have a pet dog in a city.

In one city in Switzerland, it was once against the law to slam your car door.

Mailing an entire building has been illegal in the United States since 1916, when a man mailed a forty-thousand-ton brick house across Utah to avoid high freight rates.

Pennsylvania was the first colony to legalize witchcraft.

A monkey was once tried and convicted for smoking a cigarette in South Bend, Indiana.

According to the United States Refuse Act of 1899, every industrial discharge into bodies of water since 1899 has been a crime.

Every citizen of Kentucky is required by law to take a bath at least once a year.

If you live in Michigan, it is illegal to put a skunk in your boss's desk.

In Hartford, Connecticut, you may not, under any circumstances, cross the street walking on your hands.

In Idaho, a citizen is forbidden by law to give another citizen a box of candy that weighs more than fifty pounds.

In Indiana, it is illegal to ride public transportation for at least thirty minutes after eating garlic.

In Minnesota, it is illegal for women to be dressed up as Santa Claus on city streets.

In Morrisville, Pennsylvania, women need a legal permit before they can wear lipstick in public.

In some parts of Alabama, it is illegal to carry a comb in your pocket.

In Oklahoma, it is against the law to hunt whale.

It is illegal for boys in ninth grade to grow a mustache in Binghamton, New York.

In Omaha, Nebraska, it's against the law to burp or sneeze in a church.

In Kansas, it's against the law to catch fish with your bare hands.

It's against the law to ride down the streets of Brewton, Alabama, in a motorboat.

Most burglaries occur in the winter.

THAT'S WHAT WE CALL A MILESTONE

In 1976, a Los Angeles secretary named Jannene Swift officially married a fifty-pound rock. The ceremony was witnessed by more than twenty people.

ANCIENT CIVILIZATIONS

Ancient Sybarites taught their horses to dance to music to make their parades more glamorous.

Ancient Sumerians thought the liver made blood and the heart was the center of thought.

The ancient Etruscans painted women white and men red in the wall paintings they used to decorate tombs.

Abdul Kassam Ismael, Grand Vizier of Persia in the tenth century, carried his library with him wherever he went. The 117,000 volumes were carried by 400 camels trained to walk in alphabetical order.

A two-hundred-year-old piece of Tibetan cheese was auctioned off for $1,513 in 1993.

In 1281, the Mongol army of Kublai Khan tried to invade Japan but was ravaged by a hurricane that destroyed their fleet.

The Toltecs, seventh-century native Mexicans, went to battle with wooden swords so as not to kill their enemies.

There was a pony express in Ancient Persia. Riders on this ancient circuit, wearing special colored headbands, delivered the mail across the vast stretch of Asia Minor, sometimes riding for hundreds of miles without a break.

In ancient Japan, public contests were held to see who in a town could break wind loudest and longest. Winners were awarded many prizes and received great acclaim.

🌰 UNRECORDED HISTORY

During the Cambrian period, about five hundred million years ago, a day was only 20.6 hours long.

The name of the asteroid that was believed to have killed the dinosaurs was Chixalub (pronounced *sheesh-uh-loob*).

WALK LIKE AN EGYPTIAN

Ra was the sun god of ancient Egypt.

In ancient Egypt, the apricot was called the egg of the sun, killing a cat was a crime punishable by death, and Egyptians paid their taxes in honey.

Ancient Egyptians shaved off their eyebrows to mourn the death of their cats.

Ancient Egyptians slept on pillows made of stone.

About three hundred years ago, most Egyptians died by the time they were thirty.

According to the Greek historian Herodotus, Egyptian men never became bald. The reason for this, Herodotus claimed, was that as children, Egyptian males had their heads shaved, and their scalps were continually exposed to the health-giving rays of the sun. In Egypt around 1500 B.C.E., a shaved head was considered the ultimate in feminine beauty. Egyptian women removed every hair from their heads with special gold tweezers and polished their scalps to a high sheen with buffing cloths.

Pharaoh Ramses II died in 1225 B.C.E. At the time of his death, he had fathered 111 sons and 67 daughters.

The Egyptian city of Alexandria was founded by Alexander the Great in 331 B.C.E.

The Egyptian hieroglyph for one hundred thousand is a tadpole.

Cleopatra married two of her brothers.

On some mummies that have been unwrapped, the total length of the bandages has been about 1.5 miles.

Tomb robbers believed that knocking off Egyptian sarcophagi's noses would stall curses.

A golden razor removed from King Tut's tomb was still sharp enough to be used.

IT'S GREEK TO ME

The ruins of Troy are located in Turkey.

In 290 B.C.E., Aristarchus was the first Greek astronomer to suggest that the sun was the center of the solar system.

At the height of its power, in 400 B.C.E., the Greek city of Sparta had twenty-five thousand citizens and five hundred thousand slaves.

In ancient Greece, women counted their age from the date they were married.

ROMAN HOLIDAY

High-wire acts have been enjoyed since the time of the ancient Greeks and Romans. Antique medals have been excavated from Greek islands depicting men ascending inclined cords and walking across ropes stretched between cliffs. The Greeks called these high-wire performers neurobates or oribates. In the Roman city of Herculaneum, there is a fresco representing an aerialist high on a rope, dancing and playing a flute. Sometimes Roman tightrope walkers stretched cables between the tops of two neighboring hills and performed comic dances and pantomimes while crossing.

Trivia is the Roman goddess of sorcery, hounds, and the crossroads.

Ancient Romans believed that birds mated on February 14.

Flamingo tongues were a common delicacy at Roman feasts.

Hannibal had only one eye after losing the other to a disease he caught while attacking Rome.

In ancient Rome, it was considered a sign of leadership to be born with a crooked nose.

In ancient Rome, weasels were used to catch mice.

It was decreed by law in the Roman Empire that all young maidens be fed rabbit meat because it would make them more beautiful.

Spartacus led the revolt of the Roman slaves and gladiators in 73 C.E.

The Pantheon is the largest building from ancient Rome that survives intact.

The Roman emperor Caligula made his horse a senator.

The saying "It's all fun and games until someone loses an eye" is from ancient Rome. The only rule during wrestling matches was no eye gouging. Everything else was allowed, but the only way to be disqualified was to poke someone's eyes out.

All office-seekers in the Roman Empire were obliged to wear a certain white toga for a period of one year before the election.

THE CHINA CLUB

The Chinese ideogram for *trouble* depicts two women living under one roof.

The Chinese Nationalist Golf Association claims the game is of Chinese origin (*ch'ui wan*—the ball-hitting game) from the third or second century B.C.E. There were official ordinances prohibiting a ball game with clubs in Belgium and Holland from 1360.

The Great Wall of China, which is more than 4,000 miles long, took more than 1,700 years to build. There is enough stone in the Great Wall to build an eight-foot wall encircling the globe at the equator.

IN THEIR PRIME

William Pitt, elected in 1783, was England's youngest prime minister at the age of only twenty-four.

Winston Churchill was born in a ladies' room during a dance.

"GREAT" WARS

During World War I, almost fourteen million people died in battle.

Charles de Gaulle's final words were "It hurts."

At age ninety, Peter Mustafic of Botovo, Yugoslavia, suddenly began speaking again after a silence of forty years. The Yugoslavian news agency quoted him as saying, "I just didn't want to do military service, so I stopped speaking in 1920; then I got used to it."

Prior to World War II, when guards were posted at the fence, anyone could wander right up to the front door of the White House.

Corcoran jump boots (Army jump boots) have 82 stitches on the inside of the sole and 101 stitches on the outside of the sole in honor of the 82nd and 101st Airborne Divisions' actions during World War II.

It took the United States only four days to build a ship during World War II.

During World War II, the Navajo language was used successfully as a code by the United States.

World champion chess player Reuben Fine helped the United States calculate where enemy submarines might surface based on positional probability.
During World War II, Americans tried to train bats to drop bombs.

Escape maps, compasses, and files were inserted into Monopoly game boards and smuggled into POW camps inside Germany during World War II; real money for escapees was slipped into the packs of Monopoly money.

"John has a long mustache" was the coded signal used by the French Resistance in World War II to mobilize their forces after the Allies had landed on the Normandy beaches.

Playing cards were issued to British pilots in World War II. If captured, the cards could be soaked in water and unfolded to reveal a map for escape.

The universally popular Hershey bar was used overseas during World War II as currency.

The Red Baron's real name was Manfred Von Richtofen.

SHIP OF DREAMS

Each anchor chain link on the *Titanic* was about 175 pounds.

The *Titanic* had four engines.

The *Titanic*'s radio call sign was "MGY."

The *Titanic* was running at twenty-two knots when she hit the iceberg.

Two dogs were among the *Titanic* survivors.

When the *Titanic* sunk, there were seventy-five hundred pounds of ham on it.

IT'S ALL ABOUT THE BENJAMINS

In 1968, a convention of beggars in Dacca, India, passed a resolution demanding that the minimum amount of alms be fixed at fifteen paisa (three cents).

AMERICAN HISTORY 101

More than 150 people were tried as witches and wizards in Salem, Massachusetts, in the late 1600s.

The $8 bill was designed and printed by Benjamin Franklin for the American Colonies.

During the American Revolution, many brides used to wear the color red instead of white as a symbol of rebellion.

Morocco was the first country to recognize the United States in 1789.

John Hancock was the only one of fifty signatories of the Declaration of Independence who actually signed it in July.

The first aerial photograph was taken from a balloon during the Civil War.

The Civil War was the first war in which news from the front was published within hours of its occurrence.

Robert E. Lee, of the Confederate Army, remains the only person, to date, to have graduated from the West Point military academy without a single demerit.

Robert E. Lee wore size 4½ shoe.

All the officers in the Confederate Army were given copies of *Les Misérables* by Victor Hugo to carry with them at all times. Robert E. Lee, among others, believed the book symbolized their cause. Both revolts were defeated.

Banks first used Scotch tape to mend torn currency during the Depression.

If a family had two or fewer servants in the United States in 1900, census takers recorded the family as lower middle class.

In 1954, boxers and wrestlers had to swear under oath they were not Communists before they could compete in the state of Indiana.

When Saigon fell, the signal for all Americans to evacuate was Bing Crosby's "White Christmas" being played on the radio.

THROUGH THE YEARS

In 1829, two sisters in the United States, Susan and Deborah, weighed 205 and 124 pounds although they were only five and three years old, respectively.

In 1900, the third leading cause of death was diarrhea.

In 1937, yeast sales reached $20 million a year in the United States.

IT'S THE FASHION

Before the 1800s, there were no separately designed shoes for right and left feet.

Any Russian man who wore a beard was required to pay a special tax during the time of Peter the Great.

Evidence of shoemaking exists as early as 10000 B.C.E.

In 1778, fashionable women of Paris never went out in blustery weather without a lightning rod attached to their hats.

In the marriage ceremony of the ancient Inca Indians of Peru, the couple was considered officially wed when they took off their sandals and handed them to each other.

Olive oil was used for washing the body in the ancient Mediterranean world.

Pirates thought having an earring would improve their eyesight.

Welsh mercenary bowmen in the medieval period only wore one shoe at a time.

Until the Middle Ages, underwater divers near the Mediterranean coastline collected golden strands from the pen shell, which used the strands to hold itself in place. The strands were woven into a luxury textile and made into ladies' gloves so fine that a pair could be packed into an empty walnut shell.

In Ethiopia, both males and females of the Surma tribes shave their heads as a mark of beauty.

A BAD DAY TO GET OUT OF BED

The sinking of the German vessel *Wilhelm Gustloff* is the greatest sea disaster of all time. Approximately eight thousand people drowned.

In the Great Fire of London in 1666, half of London was burned down but only six people were injured.

TGIF?

In the nineteenth century, the British Navy attempted to dispel the superstition that Friday was an unlucky day to embark on a ship. The keel of a new ship was laid on a Friday; she was named HMS *Friday*, commanded by a Captain Friday, and finally went to sea on a Friday. Neither the ship nor her crew was ever heard of again.

GIVE PEACE A CHANCE

It has been calculated that in the last 3,500 years, there have been only 230 years of peace throughout the civilized world.

Spain declared war on the United States in 1898.

The Hundred Years' War lasted 116 years.

The shortest war in history was between Zanzibar and England in 1896. Zanzibar surrendered after thirty-eight minutes.

The Spanish Inquisition once condemned the entire Netherlands to death for heresy.

Close to seven hundred thousand land mines were dug up from the banks of the Suez Canal after the 1973 war between Egypt and Israel.

NOBLE NOBEL

The Nobel Prize was first awarded in 1901. It resulted from a late change in the will of Alfred Nobel, who did not want to be remembered after his death as a propagator of violence—he invented dynamite.

RUSSIAN ROULETTE

Czar Paul I banished soldiers to Siberia for marching out of step.

Russian I. M. Chisov survived a 21,980-foot plunge out of a plane with no parachute. He landed on the steep side of a snow-covered mountain.

STUCK IN THE MIDDLE (AGES) WITH YOU

During the Middle Ages, few people were able to read or write. The clergy were virtually the only ones who could.

During the Middle Ages, it was widely believed that men had one less rib than women. This is because of the story in the Bible that Eve had been created out of Adam's rib.

Everyone believed in the Middle Ages—as Aristotle had—that the heart was the seat of intelligence.

FIRST IN LINE

The actors in the first English play to be performed in America were arrested, as acting was considered evil.

Income tax was first introduced in England in 1799 by British prime minister William Pitt.

Leif Erikson was the first European to set foot in North America, in 1000 c.e., not Columbus.

New Zealand was the first country to give women the vote, in 1890.

The first American in space was Alan B. Shepard Jr.

The Wright Brothers' first plane was called *The Bird of Prey*.

Orville Wright was involved in the first aircraft accident. His passenger, a Frenchman, was killed.

The first man ever to set foot on Antarctica was John Davis on February 7, 1821.

The first people to arrive on Iceland were Irish explorers in 795 C.E.

The first police force was established in Paris in 1667.

The first telephone book ever issued contained only fifty names. It was published in New Haven, Connecticut, by the New Haven District Telephone Company, in February 1878.

SKEWED BELIEFS

In Puritan times, to be born on a Sunday was interpreted as a sign of great sin.

In the 1700s in London, you could purchase insurance against going to hell.

In Victorian times, there was an intense fear of being buried alive. So when someone died, a small hole was dug from the casket to the surface, then a string was tied around the dead person's finger, which was then attached to a small but loud bell hung on the surface of the grave. If someone was buried alive, they could ring the bell and whoever was on duty would go and dig them up. Someone was on the duty twenty-four hours a day—hence the graveyard shift.

Long ago, the people of Nicaragua believed that if they threw beautiful young women into a volcano it would stop erupting.

In 1982, the last member of a group of people who believed the earth was hollow died.

WRONGFUL DEATH

Hrand Araklein, a Brink's car guard, was killed when $50,000 worth of quarters fell on and crushed him.

In 1911, Bobby Beach broke nearly all the bones in his body after surviving a barrel ride over Niagara Falls. Some time later in New Zealand, he slipped on a banana and died from the fall.

A fierce gust of wind blew forty-five-year-old Vittorio Luise's car into a river near Naples, Italy, in 1980. He managed to break a window, climb out, and swim to shore, where a tree blew over and killed him.

THE NEW WORLD

It costs more to buy a car today than it cost Christopher Columbus to equip and undertake three voyages to the New World.

Native Americans never actually ate turkey; killing such a timid bird was thought to indicate laziness.

Pilgrims ate popcorn at the first Thanksgiving dinner.

NATIONAL SING-A-LONGS

The national anthem of Greece has 158 verses.

The national anthem of the Netherlands, "Het Wilhelmus," is an acrostichon. The first letters of each of the fifteen verses represent the name Willem Van Nassov.

Francis Scott Key was a young lawyer who wrote the poem "The Star Spangled Banner" after being inspired by watching the Americans fight off the British attack of Baltimore during the War of 1812. The poem became the words to the national anthem.

The Netherlands and the United States both have anthems that do not mention their countries' names.

The Japanese national anthem has the oldest lyrics/text, from the ninth century, but the music is from 1880.

ROAM IF YOU WANT TO

ON THE ROAD AGAIN . . .

One hundred sixty cars can drive side by side on the Monumental Axis in Brazil, the world's widest road.

The highest motorway in England is the M62 Liverpool to Hull. At its peak, it reaches 1,221 feet above sea level over the Saddleworth Moor, the burial ground of the victims of the infamous Myra Hindley, Moors Murderer.

Built in 1697, the Frankford Avenue Bridge, which crosses Pennypack Creek in Philadelphia, is the oldest U.S. bridge in continuous use.

The Golden Gate Bridge was first opened in 1937.

IF YOU BUILD IT, THEY WILL COME

Construction on the Leaning Tower of Pisa began on August 9, 1173. There are 296 steps to the top.

The Hoover Dam was built to last two thousand years. The concrete in it will not even be fully cured for another five hundred years.

In Washington, D.C., no building can be built taller than the Washington Monument.

The Pentagon in Arlington, Virginia, has five sides, five stories, and five acres in the middle.

At one point, the Circus Maximus in Rome could hold up to 250,000 people.

Buckingham Palace has more than six hundred rooms.

The foundations of many great European cathedrals are as deep as forty to fifty feet.

At one point, the Panama Canal was going to be built in Nicaragua.

In Calcutta, 79 percent of the population lives in one-room houses.

EI-FFEL AWFUL

The Eiffel Tower was built for the 1889 World's Fair. The blueprints covered more than fourteen thousand square feet of drafting paper. The Eiffel Tower has 2.5 million rivets, and its height varies as much as six inches, depending on the temperature.

NAME GAME

Los Angeles's full name is El Pueblo de Nuestra Senora la Reina de los Angeles de Porciuncula and can be abbreviated to 6.3 percent of its size: L.A.

There is a place in Norway called Hell.

There is a resort town in New Mexico called Truth or Consequences.

There is a town in Texas called Ding Dong.

There is an airport in Calcutta named Dum Dum Airport.

There was once a town named 6 in West Virginia.

There's a cemetery town in California called Colma; its ratio of dead to living people is 750 to 1.

If you come from Manchester, you are a Manchurian.

Nova Scotia is Latin for "New Scotland."

The abbreviation ORD for Chicago's O'Hare Airport comes from the old name Orchard Field.

SOME STIFF FIGURES

If a statue of a person on a horse depicts the horse with both front legs in the air, the person died in battle; if the horse has one front leg in the air, the person died as a result of wounds received in battle; if the horse has all four legs on the ground, the person died of natural causes.

The Sphinx at Giza in Egypt is 240 feet long and carved out of limestone. Built by Pharaoh Khafre to guard the way to his pyramid, it has a lion's body and the ruler's head.

The name of the Statue of Liberty is Mother of Exiles. Printed on the book the statue is holding is "July IV, MDCCLXXVI." The statue's mouth is three feet wide.

The names of the two stone lions in front of the New York Public Library are Patience and Fortitude. They were named by the then-mayor Fiorello La-Guardia.

Worldwide, there are more statues of Joan of Arc than of anyone else. France alone has about forty thousand of them.

SCHOOL DAYS

The University of Alaska stretches across four time zones.

The main library at Indiana University sinks more than an inch every year because when it was built, engineers failed to take into account the weight of all the books that would occupy the building.

Harvard uses Yale brand locks on their buildings; Yale uses Best brand.

Harvard is the oldest university in the United States.

DO YOU HAVE THE TIME?

There are no clocks in Las Vegas gambling casinos.

The shopping mall in Abbotsford, British Columbia, has the largest water clock in North America.

The clock at the National Bureau of Standards in Washington, D.C., will gain or lose only one second in three hundred years because it uses cesium atoms.

ON DISPLAY

The Liberace Museum has a mirror-plated Rolls Royce; jewel-encrusted capes; and the largest rhinestone in the world, weighing fifty-nine pounds and measuring almost a foot in diameter.

The Future's Museum in Sweden contains a scale model of the solar system. The sun is 105 meters in diameter, and the planets range from 5 millimeters to 6 kilometers from the sun. This particular model also contains the nearest star Proxima Centauri, still to scale, situated in the Museum of Victoria . . . in Australia.

WORLD OF WONDERS

The Taj Mahal was actually built for use as a tomb. It was scheduled to be torn down in the 1830s.

It is forbidden to fly aircraft over the Taj Mahal.

Due to precipitation, for a few weeks each year K2 is taller than Mt. Everest.

If you divide the Great Pyramid's perimeter by two times its height, you get pi to the fifteenth digit.

The Great Wall stretches for 4,160 miles across North China.

The Angel Falls in Venezuela are nearly twenty times taller than Niagara Falls.

PERHAPS YOU WERE MISTAKEN

The many sights that represent the Chinese city of Beijing were built by foreigners: the Forbidden City was built by the Mongols, the Temple of Heaven by the Manchurians.

Three Mile Island is only 2.5 miles long.

I WANT TO BE A PART OF IT . . .

The amusement park Coney Island has had three of its rides designated as New York City historical landmarks.

Central Park opened in 1876. It is nearly twice the size of the entire country of Monaco.

The 102-story Empire State Building, completed in 1931, is made up of more than 10 million bricks and has 6,500 windows. It was built at a cost of $40,948,900.

CALIFORNIA DREAMIN'

Since the 1930s, the town of Corona, California, has lost all seventeen of the time capsules they originally buried.

The San Diego Zoo has the largest collection of animals in the world.

The San Francisco cable cars are the only mobile national monuments.

The largest object ever found in the Los Angeles sewer system was a motorcycle.

LOCAL CUSTOMS

If you bring a raccoon's head to the Henniker, New Hampshire, town hall, you are entitled to receive ten dollars from the town.

> There's a bathroom in Egypt where it is free to use the toilet, but you have to bring or buy your own toilet paper.

Some hotels in Las Vegas have gambling tables floating in their swimming pools.

WELL, AT LEAST WE'RE NUMBER ONE IN SOMETHING . . .

Maine is the toothpick capital of the world.

ADD IT UP

Forty-seven czars are buried within the Kremlin.

> Fifty-seven countries were involved in World War II.

There are 3,900 islands in Japan, the country of islands.

HOLY MATTERS

DIFFERING OPINIONS

Christianity has more than a billion followers. Islam is next in representation, with half this number.

The Norsemen considered the mistletoe a baleful plant that caused the death of Baldur, the shining god of youth.

In Turkey, the color of mourning is violet. In most Muslim countries and in China, it is white.

Voodoo originated in Haiti.

MONK-EYING AROUND

Ukrainian monk Dionysius Exiguus created the modern-day Christian calendar.

The monastic hours are matins, lauds, prime, tierce, sext, nones, vespers, and compline.

HOLY MOLY

The practice of exchanging presents at Christmas originated with the Romans.

The three cardinal virtues are faith, hope, and charity.

It was only after 440 C.E. that December 25 was celebrated as the birth date of Jesus Christ.

Two-thirds of Portugal was owned by the Church in the early eighteenth century.

Kerimaki Church in Finland is the world's largest church made of wood.

Las Vegas has the most chapels per capita than any other U.S. city.

St. Stephen is the patron saint of bricklayers.

IS THE POPE CATHOLIC?

Pope Adrian VI died after a fly got stuck in his throat as he was drinking from a water fountain.

The youngest pope was eleven years old.

The election of a new pope is announced to the world with white smoke.

Pope Paul IV, who was elected on May 23, 1555, was so outraged when he saw the naked bodies on the ceiling of the Sistine Chapel that he ordered Michelangelo to paint clothes on them.

CAN YOU BELIEVE IT?

A young shepherd boy discovered the Dead Sea Scrolls at Qumran, Jordan, in 1947.

Snow angels originated from medieval Jewish mystics who practiced rolling in the snow to purge themselves of evil urges.

BUDDHA-OLOGY

Contrary to popular belief, there are almost no Buddhists in India, nor have there been for about a thousand years. Although Buddhism was founded in India around 470 B.C.E. and developed there at an early date, it was uprooted from India between the seventh and twelfth centuries C.E. and today exists almost exclusively outside the country, primarily in Sri Lanka, Japan, and Indochina.

A temple in Sri Lanka is dedicated to one of the Buddha's teeth.

HINDU WHO?

Hindu men once believed it to be unlucky to marry a third time. They could avoid misfortune by marrying a tree first. The tree (the third wife) was then burned, freeing the man to marry again.

Some husbands and wives in India who desire children whisper their wish in the ear of a sacred cow.

On the stone temples of Madura in southern India, there are more than thirty million carved images of gods and goddesses.

BUSINESS RELATIONS

BRANDING THE COW

A single share of Coca-Cola stock purchased in 1919, when the company went public, would have been worth ten million dollars today.

NERF, the popular foam children's toy company, doesn't actually stand for anything.

Nestlé is the largest company in Switzerland, yet more than 98 percent of its revenue comes from outside the country.

THEY'RE IN THE MONEY

Japan's currency is the most difficult to counterfeit.

John D. Rockefeller was the first billionaire in the United States.

Howard Hughes once made half a billion dollars in one day. In 1966, he received a bank draft for $546,549,171 in return for his 75 percent holdings in TWA.

Ted Turner owns 5 percent of New Mexico.

Organized crime is estimated to account for 10 percent of the United States' national income.

LOSE SOME TO MAKE SOME

It takes about sixty-three thousand trees to make the newsprint for the average Sunday edition of *The New York Times*.

The average bank cashier loses $310 a year.

THE JOB MARKET

Sixty percent of big-firm executives say the cover letter is as important as or more important than the résumé itself when you're looking for a new job.

The largest employer in the world is the Indian railway system, employing more than a million people.

SELLER'S MARKET

The sale of vodka makes up 10 percent of Russian government income.

In most advertisements, the time displayed on a watch is 10:10.

THE SPORTING GOODS

YOU'RE OUT!

Sixty-eight million people go to Major League baseball games each year.

A baseball has exactly 108 stitches.

Babe Ruth wore a cabbage leaf under his hat to keep his head cool. He changed it every two innings.

Bank robber John Dillinger played professional baseball.

Baseball games between college teams have been played since the Civil War.

Baseball was the first sport to be pictured on the cover of *Sports Illustrated* magazine.

Baseball's home plate is seventeen inches wide.

Before 1859, baseball umpires used to sit in rocking chairs behind home plate.

It takes about eight seconds to make a baseball bat in a baseball bat factory.

The first formal rules for playing baseball required the winning team to score twenty-one runs.

NOTHING BUT NET

Basketball was invented by Canadian James Naismith in 1891.

The theme song of the Harlem Globetrotters is "Sweet Georgia Brown."

RUN ON

In 1936, American track star Jesse Owens beat a racehorse over a one-hundred-yard course. The horse was given a head start.

Sprinters on track teams started taking a crouching start in 1908.

The expression "getting someone's goat" is based on the custom of keeping a goat in the stable with a racehorse as the horse's companion. The goat becomes a settling influence for the Thoroughbred. If you owned a competing horse and were not above some dirty business, you could steal your rival's goat (it's been done) to upset the other horse and make it run a poor race.

Anise is the scent on the artificial rabbit that is used in greyhound races.

BEND IT LIKE BECKHAM

Soccer is played in more countries than any other sport.

Soccer legend Pele's real name is Edson Arantes do Nascimento.

BLUE 42! HUT!

Green Bay Packers backup quarterback Matt Hasselbeck has been struck by lightning twice in his life.

It takes three thousand cows to supply the NFL with enough leather for a year's supply of footballs.

An American football has four seams.

The Super Bowl is broadcast in 182 countries. That is more than 88 percent of the countries in the world.

When the University of Nebraska Cornhuskers play football at home, the stadium becomes the state's third largest city.

FORE!

Rudyard Kipling, living in Vermont in the 1890s, invented the game of snow golf. He painted his golf balls red so he could locate them in the snow.

Americans spend more than $630 million a year on golf balls.

Before 1850, golf balls were made of leather and stuffed with feathers.

Golfing great Ben Hogan's famous reply when asked how to improve one's game was, "Hit the ball closer to the hole."

In the United States, there are more than fifteen thousand golf courses.

Many Japanese golfers carry hole-in-one insurance, because it is traditional in Japan to share one's good luck by sending gifts to all your friends when you get an ace. The price for what the Japanese term "an albatross" can often reach $10,000.

Pro golfer Wayne Levi was the first PGA pro to win a tournament using a colored (orange) ball. He did it in the Hawaiian Open.

Twelve new golf holes are constructed every day.

The only person ever to play golf on the moon was Alan Shepard. His golf ball was never found.

The Tom Thumb golf course was the first miniature golf course in the United States. It was built it 1929 in Chattanooga, Tennessee, by John Garnet Carter.

The United States Golf Association was founded in 1894 as the governing body of golf in the United States.

The youngest golfer recorded to have shot a hole-in-one is five-year-old Coby Orr of Littleton, Colorado, on the 103-yard fifth hole at the Riverside Golf Course in San Antonio, Texas, in 1975.

A regulation golf ball has 336 dimples.

Two golf clubs claim to be the first established in the United States: the Foxberg Golf Club in Clarion County, Pennsylvania (1887), and St. Andrews Golf Club of Yonkers, New York (1888).

KNOCK OUT

Boxing is considered the easiest sport for gamblers to fix.

Boxing rings are so called because they used to be round.

In 1985, Mike Tyson started boxing professionally at age eighteen.

Four men in the history of boxing have been knocked out in the first eleven seconds of the first round.

OLYMPIC FANFARE

Canada is the only country not to win a gold medal in the Summer Olympic Games while hosting the event.

Only two countries have participated in every modern Olympic Games: Greece and Australia.

The 1900 Olympics were held in Paris, France.

Tug-of-war was an Olympic event between 1900 and 1920.

The five Olympic rings represent the continents.

Olympic badminton rules say that the birdie has to have exactly fourteen feathers.

The city of Denver was chosen to host and then refused the 1976 Winter Olympics.

FISHING FOR SWIMMERS

A top freestyle swimmer achieves a speed of only five miles per hour. Fish, in contrast, have been clocked at sixty-eight miles per hour.

Captain Matthew Webb of England was the first to swim the English Channel using the breaststroke.

SURPRISING SPORTS

In the United States, more Frisbee discs are sold each year than baseballs, basketballs, and footballs combined.

Kite-flying is a professional sport in Thailand.

There are at least two sports in which the team has to move backward to win—tug-of-war and rowing.

Badminton used to be called "Poona."

PIN AND CONQUER

The national sport of Japan is sumo wrestling.

Morihei Ueshiba, founder of Aikido, once pinned a sumo wrestler using only a single finger.

Nearly all sumo wrestlers have flat feet and big bottoms.

The 1912 Greco-Roman wrestling match in Stockholm between Finn Alfred Asikainen and Russian Martin Klein lasted more than eleven hours.

LORDS OF THE ICE

A hockey puck is one inch thick.

Canada imports about 850 Russian-made hockey sticks on an average day.

Professional hockey players skate at average speeds of twenty to twenty-five miles per hour.

ON STRIKES

Three consecutive strikes in bowling are called a turkey.

Tokyo has the world's largest bowling alley.

The bowling ball was invented in 1862.

FIRST CONTACT

The game of squash originated in the United Kingdom.

Australian Rules Football was originally designed to give cricketers something to play during the off- season.

Karate actually originated in India.

DANGEROUS GAMES

The only bone not broken so far during any ski accident is one located in the inner ear.

AND THE HEAVYWEIGHT CHAMPION OF THE WORLD IS . . .

Sports Illustrated has the largest sports magazine circulation.

THROW THE GAME

A forfeited game in baseball is recorded as a 9–0 score. In football, it is recorded as a 1–0 score.

TEAM SPIRIT

In the four professional major North American sports (baseball, basketball, football, and hockey), only eight teams' nicknames do not end with "s." These teams are the Miami Heat, the Utah Jazz, the Orlando Magic, the Boston Red Sox, the Chicago White Sox, the Colorado Avalanche, the Tampa Bay Lightning, and the Minnesota Wild.

BE FLEXIBLE

Pole vault poles used to be stiff. Now they bend, which allows the vaulter to go much higher.

Scientifically Speaking

AMAZING DISCOVERIES

A device invented as a primitive steam engine by the Greek engineer Hero, about the time of the birth of Christ, is used today as a rotating lawn sprinkler.

Construction workers' hard hats were first invented and used in the building of the Hoover Dam in 1933.

Leonardo da Vinci invented the concept of the parachute, but his design was fatally flawed in that it did not allow air to pass through the top of the chute. Therefore, the chute would not fall straight, but would tilt to the side, lose its air, and plummet. He also invented the scissors.

Thomas Edison, the inventor of the lightbulb, was afraid of the dark.

A WEATHER EYE

A normal raindrop falls at about seven miles per hour.

A downburst is a downward-blowing wind that some-times comes blasting out of a thunderstorm. The dam-age looks like tornado damage, because the wind can be as strong as an F2 tornado, but debris is blown straight away from a point on the ground, not lifted into the air and transported downwind.

A wind with a speed of seventy-four miles per hour or more is designated a hurricane.

An inch of snow falling evenly on 1 acre of ground is equivalent to about 2,715 gallons of water.

At any given time, there are eighteen hundred thunder-storms in progress over the earth's atmosphere.

A cubic mile of fog is made up of less than a gallon of water.

The two hottest months at the equator are March and September.

A rainbow can only occur when the sun is forty degrees or less above the horizon.

Meteorologists claim they're right 85 percent of the time.

ROCKETMEN

Astronauts in orbit around the earth can see the wakes of ships.

Buzz Aldrin's mother's maiden name was Moon.

Buzz Aldrin was the first man to pee his pants on the moon.

Neil Armstrong stepped on the moon with his left foot first.

The first man to return safely from space was Yuri Gagarin.

Three astronauts manned each *Apollo* flight.

The *Saturn V* moon rocket consumed fifteen tons of fuel per second.

The *Apollo 11* had only twenty seconds of fuel left when it landed.

The external tank on the space shuttle is not painted.

A manned rocket can reach the moon in less time than it took a stagecoach to travel the length of England.

Valentina Tereshkova was the first woman to enter space.

A SPACE ODYSSEY

All the stars in the Milky Way revolve around the center of the galaxy every two hundred million years.

Astronomers classify stars by their spectra.

Three stars make up Orion's belt.

French astronomer Adrien Auzout once considered building a telescope that was one thousand feet long in the 1600s. He thought the magnification would be so great he would see animals on the moon.

A neutron star has such a powerful gravitational pull that it can spin on its axis in one-thirtieth of a second without tearing itself apart. A pulsar is a neutron star, and it gets its energy from its rotation.

Stars come in different colors; hot stars give off blue light, and the cooler stars give off red light.

Earth is traveling through space at 660,000 miles per hour.

🌰 MOON RIVER

A full moon always rises at sunset.

A full moon is nine times brighter than a half moon.

February 1865 is the only month in recorded history not to have a full moon.

Carolyn Shoemaker has discovered thirty-two comets and approximately three hundred asteroids.

Any free-moving liquid in outer space will form itself into a sphere because of its surface tension.

The total quantity of energy in the universe is constant.

If you attempted to count the stars in a galaxy at a rate of one every second, it would take around three thousand years to count them all.

A syzygy occurs when three astronomical bodies line up.

The sixteenth-century astronomer Tycho Brahe lost his nose in a duel with one of his students over a mathematical computation. He wore a silver replacement nose for the rest of his life.

HERE COMES THE SUN

By weight, the sun is 70 percent hydrogen; 28 percent helium; 1.5 percent carbon, nitrogen, and oxygen; and 0.5 percent all other elements.

It takes eight and a half minutes for light to get from the sun to Earth. All totaled, the sunlight that strikes Earth at any given moment weighs as much as an ocean liner.

Galileo became totally blind just before his death. This is probably because of his constant gazing at the sun through his telescope.

Sunbeams that shine down through clouds are called crepuscular rays.

THE ELECTRIC SLIDE

One of the first lightbulbs was a thread of sheep's wool coated with carbon.

A bolt of lightning can strike the earth with a force as great as one hundred million volts and generates temperatures five times hotter than those found on the sun's surface.

You are more likely to lose your hearing than any of the other senses if you are hit by lightning.

TECHNOLOGICALLY ADVANCED

The first computer ever made was called ENIAC. A silicon chip a quarter-inch square has the capacity of the original 1949 ENIAC computer, which occupied a city block.

In 1961, MIT student Steve Russell created Spacewars, the first interactive computer game, on a Digital PDP-1 (Programmed Data Processor-1) mainframe computer. Limited by the computer technology of the time, ASCII text characters were the "graphics" and people could only play the game on a device that took up the floor space of a small house.

In 1949, forecasting the relentless march of science, *Popular Mechanics* said computers in the future may weigh no more than five tons.

Back in the mid to late 1980s, an IBM-compatible computer wasn't considered 100 percent compatible unless it could run Microsoft's Flight Simulator.

Toronto was the first city in the world with a computerized traffic signal system.

The first product Motorola started to develop was a record player for automobiles. At that time, the most well-known player on the market was the Victrola, so they called themselves Motorola.

When CBS broadcast the first television show in color, no one other than CBS owned a color television set.

In 1977, Cairo only had 208,000 telephones and no telephone books.

THE THIRD "R"

All snow crystals are hexagonal.

An enneahedron is solid with nine faces.

The billionth digit of pi is nine.

René Descartes came up with the theory of coordinate geometry by looking at a fly walk across a tiled ceiling.

LEAVING ON A JET PLANE

A jumbo jet uses four thousand gallons of fuel to take off.

A Boeing 747's wingspan is longer than the distance of the Wright Brothers' first flight.

The tail section of an airplane gives the bumpiest ride.

The condensed water vapor left by jets in the sky is called a contrail.

American Airlines saved $40,000 in 1987 by eliminating one olive from each salad served in first class.

The Boeing 747 has been in commercial service since 1970.

The shortest intercontinental commercial flight in the world is from Gibraltar in Europe to Tangier in Africa at a distance of thirty-four miles and a flight time of twenty minutes.

I FEEL THE EARTH MOVE

April is Earthquake Preparedness Month. For a little added incentive, consider this: the most powerful earthquake to strike the United States occurred in 1811 in New Madrid, Missouri. The quake shook more than one million square miles and was felt as far as one thousand miles away.

A REAL GEM

A large, flawless emerald is worth more than a similarly large flawless diamond.

Gold was the first metal to be discovered. South Africa produces two-thirds of the world's gold. All the gold produced in the past five hundred years, if melted, could be compressed into a fifty-foot cube. A lump of pure gold the size of a Matchbox car can be flattened into a sheet the size of a tennis court. India has the world's largest stock of privately hoarded gold.

Diamonds are composed of just one chemical element, carbon. The color of diamond dust is black. According to the Gemological Institute of America, up until 1896, India was the only source of diamonds in the world.

GREEN THUMB

Bamboo (the world's tallest grass) can grow up to 35 inches in a day.

It takes the insect-eating Venus flytrap plant only half a second to shut its trap on its prey. The Venus flytrap can eat a whole cheeseburger.

The Siberian larch accounts for more than 20 percent of all the world's trees.

The Sitka spruce is Britain's most commonly planted tree.

The Saguaro Cactus, found in the southwestern United States, doesn't grow branches until it is seventy-five years old.

The leaves of the Victorian water lily are sometimes more than six feet in diameter.

The bark of a redwood tree is fireproof. Fires that occur in a redwood forest take place inside the trees.

Orchids are grown from seeds so small it would take thirty thousand to weigh as much as one grain of wheat.

It takes one fifteen- to twenty-year-old tree to produce seven hundred paper grocery bags.

One ragweed plant can release as many as one billion grains of pollen.

LET'S GET PHYSIC-AL

A cesium atom in an atomic clock beats 9,192,631,770 times a second.

A temperature of 70 million degrees Celsius was generated at Princeton University in 1978. This was during a fusion experiment and is the highest man-made temperature ever.

During the time that the atomic bomb was being hatched by the United States at Alamogordo, New Mexico, applicants for routine jobs like janitors were disqualified if they could read. Illiteracy was a job requirement. The reason: the authorities did not want their garbage or other papers read.

The radioactive substance Americanium-241 is used in many smoke detectors.

The average life of a nuclear plant is forty years.

CHEMICAL REACTIONS

German chemist Hennig Brand discovered phosphorus while he was examining urine.

A "creep" is a metallurgical term for when something that is normally very strong bends because of gravity. This happens to many metals at high temperatures, where they won't melt but they will creep.

All organic compounds contain carbon.

Almost all the helium that exists in the world today is from natural gas wells in the United States.

Hydrogen is the most common atom in the universe.

Mercury is the only metal that is liquid at room temperature.

Methane gas can often be seen bubbling up from the bottom of ponds. It is produced by the decomposition of dead plants and animals in the mud.

The ashes of the metal magnesium are heavier than magnesium itself.

There are five trillion trillion atoms in one pound of iron.

The densest substance on Earth is the metal osmium.

The metal part at the end of a pencil is 20 percent sulfur.

The 111th element is known as unnilenilenium.

The U.S. Bureau of Standards says that the electron is the fastest thing in the world.

The shockwave from a nitroglycerine explosion travels at seventeen thousand miles per hour.

Marie Curie, the Nobel Prize–winning scientist who discovered radium, died on July 4, 1934, of radiation poisoning.

CHILLY WATERS

H_2O expands as it freezes and contracts as it melts, displacing the exact same amount of fluid in either state. So if the northern ice cap did melt, it would cause absolutely no rise in the level of the ocean.

Hot water is heavier than cold.

An iceberg contains more heat than a match.

WEIRD SCIENCE

One hundred seven incorrect medical procedures will be performed by the end of the day today.

Because of the rotation of the earth, an object can be thrown farther if it is thrown west.

Two and five are the only prime numbers that end in two or five.

Fifty-one percent of turns are right turns.

If you toss a penny 10,000 times, it will not be heads 5,000 times but more like 4,950. The head picture weighs more, so it ends up on the bottom.

If you yelled for eight years, seven months, and six days, you would have produced enough sound energy to heat one cup of coffee.

The strength of early lasers was measured in Gillettes, the number of blue razor blades a given beam could puncture.

The tip of a bullwhip moves so fast that it breaks the sound barrier; the crack of the whip is actually a tiny sonic boom.

Clouds fly higher during the day than at night.

Moisture, not air, causes superglue to dry.

Iron nails cannot be used in oak because the acid in the wood corrodes them.

Bacteria, the tiniest free-living cells, are so small that a single drop of liquid contains as many as fifty million of them.

Life on Earth probably developed in an oxygen-free atmosphere. Even today there are microorganisms that can live only in the absence of oxygen.

Stainless steel was discovered by accident in 1913.

SYNTHETIC MATERIALS

Edmonton, Canada, was the first city in North America with a population of less than one million to open a Light Rail Transit System, in 1978.

Russia built more than ten thousand miles of railroad between 1896 and 1900.

The U.S. standard railroad gauge (the distance between rails) is 4 feet, 8.5 inches.

A fully loaded supertanker traveling at normal speed takes at least twenty minutes to stop.

The first American submarine was built around 1776.

Robots in Japan pay union dues.

The metal instrument used in shoe stores to measure feet is called the Brannock device.

The CN Tower in Toronto is the tallest free-standing structure in the world.

Man releases more than a billion tons of pollutants into the earth's atmosphere every year.

EXPERT TIMING

The smallest unit of time is the yoctosecond.

Twenty years make up a vicennial period.

At room temperature, the average air molecule travels at the speed of a rifle bullet.

A jiffy is an actual unit of time: one-hundredth of a second. Thus the saying, "I will be there in a jiffy!"

SEVEN UP

THE MAGNIFICENT SEVEN

Charles Bronson—Bernordo
Yul Brynner—Chris
Horst Buchholz—Chico
James Coburn—Britt
Brad Dexter—Harry
Steve McQueen—Vin
Robert Vaughn—Lee

THE SEVEN DWARFS

Bashful
Doc
Dopey
Grumpy
Happy
Sleepy
Sneezy

THE SEVEN DEADLY SINS

Avarice
Envy
Gluttony
Lust
Pride
Sloth
Wrath

THE SEVEN WONDERS OF THE ANCIENT WORLD

Great Pyramid of Giza
Hanging Gardens of Babylon
Mausoleum of Halicarnassus
Temple of Artemis at Ephesus
Colossus of Rhodes
Pharos (Lighthouse) of Alexandria
Statue of Zeus at Olympia

THE SEVEN VIRTUES

Justice
Fortitude
Prudence
Temperance
Faith
Hope
Charity

THE SEVEN SEAS

North Atlantic Ocean
South Atlantic Ocean
North Pacific Ocean
South Pacific Ocean
Indian Ocean
Arctic Ocean
Antarctic Ocean

THE SEVEN SIZES OF GRAND PIANO

Baby Grand—five feet, eight inches
Living Room Grand—five feet, ten inches
Professional Grand—six feet
Drawing Room Grand—6 feet, four inches
Parlor Grand—6 feet, eight inches
Half Concert Grand—seven feet, four inches
Concert Grand—eight feet, eleven inches or
    longer

THE SEVEN CHILDREN OF BARON VON TRAPP OF <u>THE SOUND OF MUSIC</u> FAME

Liesel
Friedrich
Louisa

Brigitta
Kurt
Marta
Gretl

THE SEVEN COLORS OF THE RAINBOW

Red
Orange
Yellow
Green
Blue
Indigo
Violet

THE SEVEN DAYS OF CREATION

Created heaven and earth; day and night.
Divided heaven from earth.
Created the land, the sea, and vegetation.
Created the sun, the moon, and the stars.
Created creatures great and small.
Created mankind.
Sanctified the seventh day as the day of rest.

THE SEVEN HILLS OF ROME

Palatine
Capitoline
Quirinal
Viminal
Esquiline
Caelian
Aventine

THE SEVEN AGES OF MAN
(ACCORDING TO SHAKESPEARE)

The Infant
The Schoolboy
The Lover
The Soldier
The Justice
The Pantaloon
The Second Childhood

THE SEVEN JAPANESE GODS
OF LUCK

Bishamon
Daikoku
Ebisu
Fukurokuju
Jurojin

Hotei
Benten

THE SEVEN DESTINATIONS OF THE CROSBY AND HOPE ON-THE-ROAD MOVIES (1940 TO 1962)

Rio
Hong Kong
Singapore
Zanzibar
Morocco
Utopia
Bali

THE SEVEN IONIAN ISLANDS

Corfu
Cephalonia
Zacynthus
Leucas
Ithaca
Cythera
Paxos

THE SEVEN MEDIEVAL CHAMPIONS OF CHRISTENDOM

St. George—England

St. Denis—France

St. James—Spain

St. Anthony—Italy

St. Andrew—Scotland

St. Patrick—Ireland

St. David—Wales

THE SEVEN GIFTS OF THE HOLY SPIRIT

Wisdom

Understanding

Counsel

Fortitude

Knowledge

Piety

Fear of the Lord

THE SEVEN SISTERS

The seven stars in the Taurus constellation visible to the naked eye, named after the daughters of the Titan Atlas and the Oceanid Pleione in Greek mythology.

Alcyone

Maia

Electra

Merope

Taygete

Celaeno

Asterope

THE SEVEN SPIRITUAL WORKS OF MERCY

To convert the sinner.

To instruct the ignorant.

To counsel those in doubt.

To comfort those in sorrow.

To bear wrongs patiently.

To forgive injuries.

To pray for the living and the dead.

THE SEVEN CORPORAL WORKS OF MERCY

To tend the sick.

To feed the hungry.

To give drink to the thirsty.

To clothe the naked.

To harbor the stranger.

To minister to prisoners.

To bury the dead.

STATISTICS

PLANES, TRAINS, AND AUTOMOBILES

Traveling by air is the safest means of transportation. More people are killed by donkeys annually than are killed in plane crashes.

A car is stolen every six minutes in the United States.

The record for the world's worst driver is a toss-up between two candidates: first, a seventy-five-year-old man who received ten traffic tickets, drove on the wrong side of the road four times, committed four hit-and-run offenses, and caused six accidents—all within twenty minutes on October 15, 1966. Second, a sixty-two-year-old woman who failed her driving test forty times before passing it in August 1970 (by that time, she could no longer afford to buy a car).

Less than 1 percent of all road accidents in Canada involve a moose.

It would take more than 150 years to drive a car to the sun.

More than 10 percent of all the salt produced annually in the world is used to de-ice American roads.

DAILY ROUTINE

Children between the ages of two and seven color, on average, for twenty-eight minutes every day.

The average adult spends about twelve minutes in the shower.

The average four-year-old child asks more than four hundred questions a day.

The average person speaks about 31,500 words per day.

The average person spends about two years on the phone in a lifetime.

The average person will spend two weeks over their lifetime waiting for the traffic lights to change.

🐿 LEISURE TIME

Seventy percent of all boats sold are used in fishing.

Ninety percent of women who walk into a department store immediately turn to the right.

In Japan, 20 percent of all publications sold are comic books.

The longest kiss on record lasted 130 hours, 2 minutes.

The world record for carrying a milk bottle on your head is twenty-four miles.

Halifax, Nova Scotia, has the largest number of bars per capita of anywhere else in the world.

COULD THERE BE A CONNECTION?

About one out of every seventy people who pick their nose actually eats their boogers.

Ninety-five percent of food poisoning cases are never reported.

CAUSE OF DEATH

You're more likely to be killed by a Champagne cork than a poisonous spider.

Odds of being killed by a dog are one in seven hundred thousand.

Odds of being killed by a tornado are one in two million.

Odds of being killed by falling out of bed are one in two million.

WEDDED BLISS

Two out of five husbands tell their wives daily that they love them.

Thirty-five percent of the people who use personal ads for dating are already married.

Nobody has yet explained satisfactorily why couples who marry in January, February, and March tend to have the highest divorce rates.

Experienced waitresses say that married men tip better than unmarried men.

REPEAT OFFENDERS

Fifty percent of bank robberies take place on Fridays.

Chances that a burglary in the United States will be solved: one in seven.

PUBLIC OPINION

One out of four people do not know what their astrological sign is.

Fifty percent of teenage boys say they would rather be rich than smart.

Sixty-nine percent of men say they would rather break up with a girl in private than in public.

Seven percent of Americans think Elvis is alive.

Nine percent of Americans report having been in the presence of a ghost.

Only 55 percent of Americans know that the sun is a star.

Eighty-two percent of the world's population believes in an afterlife.

BUT CAN YOU REMEMBER
THEIR NAMES?

Assuming Rudolph was in front, there are 40,320 ways to rearrange the other eight reindeer.

BABY BOOMS

About two hundred babies are born worldwide every minute.

August is the month when most babies are born.

The world record for most children to one mother is sixty-nine children.

You share a birthday with at least nine million other people in the world.

There are about fifteen thousand people in the United States over the age of one hundred.

PLAYING IT SAFE

Statistically, the safest age of life is ten years old.

Summer is statistically the most hazardous season.

You are more likely to get attacked by a cow than a shark.

In the next seven days, eight hundred Americans will be injured by their jewelry.

THIS WAS ALL FOR NOTHING . . .

Approximately 97 percent of all statistics are made up.